MAD
TOFFS

'Eventually he picked up the speaking tube that connected him to his chauffeur and said: "How is it that I have never been informed that the lower orders have such white skins?"'

MAD TOFFS

The British Upper Classes at Their Best – and Worst

Patrick Scrivenor
Illustrated by Phil O'Farrell

metro

First published by Metro Publishing,
an imprint of
John Blake Publishing Limited
3 Bramber Court, 2 Bramber Road
London W14 9PB

www.johnblakepublishing.co.uk

www.facebook.com/johnblakebooks 🅕
twitter.com/jblakebooks 🅴

First published in hardback in 2016

ISBN: 978-1-78418-767-5

British Library Cataloguing-in-Publication Data:

A catalogue record for this book is available from the British Library.

Design by www.envydesign.co.uk

Printed in Great Britain by CPI Group (UK) Ltd

1 3 5 7 9 10 8 6 4 2

Papers used by John Blake Publishing are natural, recyclable products made
from wood grown in sustainable forests. The manufacturing processes
conform to the environmental regulations of the country of origin.

Every attempt has been made to contact the relevant copyright-holders,
but some were unobtainable. We would be grateful if the appropriate
people could contact us.

CONTENTS

'When shooting, he divided his beard into two plaits, which he tied behind his neck, out of the way of the stock of his gun.'

INTRODUCTION

This book is a record of the British upper classes – and a few others – at their best (sometimes their worst), displaying a sort of unhinged blitheness of manner that leads them to say and do strangely unexpected things. It is a quality of innocent insolence, or maybe guileless arrogance, that belongs only to the very rich, the very privileged and the very idle. Other writers have referred to it as the 'Higher Lunacy', and perhaps lunacy, or near lunacy, is the only connecting thread in this varied collection. There will be many to say that I have strayed outside the boundaries of the upper class. As defined by the writer Anthony Trollope, I have. He referred to 'the top ten thousand', meaning the titled and untitled owners of land and their immediate families. They are represented here, God knows, in heaping measure, but they do not represent the whole of the upper class. This extends from the royal family at the top, down through the titled aristocracy, untitled landowners, the high functionaries of state, embracing on the way the whole of the public school- and Oxbridge-educated class, the officer class of the services, and includes all those who have been able to force their way to prominence by talent, money, or industry. This latitude was made possible by the invention, during the eighteenth and nineteenth centuries, of the idea of a 'gentleman', and it continues to be possible today because no one knows exactly what a gentleman is.

'It is a line,' said Evelyn Waugh, 'that everybody draws immediately below his own heels.' Another definition is that 'no gentleman lives north of the park'. (Evelyn Waugh was born in Highgate, not only north of the park, for heaven's sake, but north of Hampstead Heath as well.) The idea of a 'gentleman' was very useful to the emergent middle classes of the nineteenth century. It enabled them, given access to the right education, to 'identify with' the old upper class, and even to some extent to merge into it at the upper end of their new-gotten wealth. But it also enabled them to look down on what they regarded as the raffish and immoral side of upper-class life. You could be a gentleman without being a noble, but you could also be a noble without being a gentleman.

In this way the fifth Earl of Lonsdale could be called – by those with far fewer pretensions to rank – 'almost an emperor; not quite a gentleman'. This is an interesting distinction because it refers not to any moral turpitude in the Earl's lifestyle, but to its lavish ostentation. In this view a gentleman did not habitually smoke the fattest cigars, still less take a special train for himself, his whole domestic staff, his foxhounds, his hunters, and a secretary to stay awake and tip the stationmaster of each station as they went through, on his annual migration from one country seat to another. He was known as the Yellow Earl because of his fondness for the colour. All his retainers were dressed in yellow liveries. He had a fleet of yellow motor cars, a pack of yellow dogs, and a hothouse growing yellow gardenias for his daily buttonhole. The Lowther arms were reproduced every day in coloured chalks in the sand of his courtyard at Lowther Castle to impress his many guests – including Kaiser Wilhelm II. He endowed the boxing trophy, the Lonsdale Belt, and was a patron of hunting, racing and many other sports. Before he inherited he was involved in a scandal because of his conspicuously public affairs with the actresses Lillie Langtry and Violet Cameron. No lesser personage than Queen Victoria advised him to leave the country, and he undertook a journey of Arctic exploration in Canada on which he nearly died. About a hundred guides and porters did die. It is difficult to imagine that he cared much about being thought a gentleman.

Others did. Lord Curzon fretted continually on the subject.

'Gentlemen do not take soup at luncheon.'

Can this be so? I would have thought that the clubs of London were awash with soup from twelve to two-thirty. He said this when presented with the proposed menu for a luncheon at Balliol College to celebrate Queen Mary's honorary degree. He was vexed that he had not been consulted, and seized on any excuse to strike out the soup. So we may assume that this was Pique rather than Protocol. But even stranger preoccupations surfaced in the proconsular mind.

'Gentlemen never wear brown in London.'

Really? No brown underpants? No brown socks? Does it matter? And anyway surely Curzon, of all people, felt himself superior to the shibboleths of gentility? Not so Evelyn Waugh.

'Impotence and sodomy are socially OK, but birth control is flagrantly middle class.'

He was of course speaking as a Catholic, which may have coloured his view.

'No real English gentleman, in his secret soul, was ever sorry for the death of a political economist.'

INTRODUCTION

No. This is not Waugh, though it might well be. It is Walter Bagehot, and he should know, having been a political economist himself. But however much the gentleman may thirst for the blood of economists, his appearance should always be impeccable. Here is the founder of the Boy Scout Movement, Lord Baden-Powell, warning his young charges against the affectation of waxed moustaches: 'It often means vanity, and sometimes drink.'

And a gentleman's behaviour must be impeccable too: 'A gentleman is one who can play the accordion, but doesn't.'

An unattributed remark: certainly not Baden-Powell, who would have played an accordion at the drop of his scouting hat. And another strange convention to observe, also anonymous: 'A gentleman is one who never swears at his wife when ladies are present.'

He is also expected to be some sort of genius with the carving knife: 'A gentleman is one who can make a grouse do for six.' (Nigel Nicolson, son of Harold Nicolson.) It is no surprise that the umbrella plays a potent part in this myth: 'A gentleman never unfurls his umbrella.' This is the judgement of Lieutenant-Colonel A. D. Wintle, who loved his umbrella so much that he even slept with it for many years of his life. It was clearly an aid to manhood because he captured a German platoon single-handed in the First World War.

That is another aspect of the gentleman – he is expected to be warlike, even if his only weapon is an umbrella.

There are countless other shibboleths and constraints that mark the gentleman. He never hunts south of the Thames. He never shoots on Saturdays. And he always leaves the bottom button of his waistcoat open: a tribute to Edward VII – 'Tum-Tum' – who had no option but to leave it open. It persists even now.

Small wonder that no one quite knows what a gentleman is. Let us reconstruct him. He never ventures north of Hyde Park. He is not ostentatious, but this presents difficulties. Nothing marks a chap more conspicuously than an accordion that he refuses to play. He is never to be seen in brown clothes in London, and helplessly thirsts for soup at midday. When not impotent he is given to sodomy, and harbours an entirely understandable longing to kill an economist. He *never* waxes his moustache, and can dismember a grouse with surgical skill – but only if he can swear at his wife afterwards. His hunters have never sniffed the keen air of Surrey, Kent and Sussex, and his guns are resolutely cased on Saturdays. His weskit remains incompletely fastened, and his umbrella implacably furled.

It is also important to note that, after a certain date, a gentleman did not wear a beard. Lord Hugh Cecil, whom we shall encounter later in connection with unexploded bombs, was quite clear about this. He taxed his cousin, Algernon Cecil, with sporting a beard, and in self-extenuation Algernon replied 'Our Lord wore a beard'. 'Our Lord,' Hugh Cecil sternly replied, 'was not a gentleman.'

This seems to clinch the matter, but it hasn't really helped. Perhaps it would be easier if we used some form of analogy. It used to be said that you could classify all British Prime Ministers as either Bishops or Bookies. Let's give it a go, starting in 1945. Attlee, definitely a Bishop. Churchill, unmistakably a Bookie. Eden, a Bishop. Macmillan, a Bookie. Douglas-Home, a Bishop. Wilson, a Bookie. Heath, a Bishop. Callaghan, a Bishop. Thatcher, a Bookie in pursuit of a defaulting punter. Major, a Bishop. Blair – Ah! Here we strike a difficulty; unmistakably both Bookie and Bishop. Brown, a Bookie. Cameron, a Bishop – in a very real sense.

But was any of them a gentleman? After an embarrassing silence up comes the hesitant suggestion – 'Perhaps Sir Alec Douglas-Home.'

In any case it is clear that the upper class is a broad church. It merges imperceptibly into something called the upper middle class, and it is often impossible to distinguish a member of the upper middle class going up, and a member of the old upper class coming down. I shall not even try, and I shall merely spread my net wherever the fishing seems good.

The memoirs of the good and great, and particularly those of their hangers-on, exhale a quality of vacuous blandness that is almost impossible to define, but which has been brilliantly parodied by the Canadian writer and humorist, Stephen Leacock. I have no misgivings about quoting him at some length:

AN ANECDOTE OF THE DUKE OF STRATHYTHAN

Lady Ranelagh writes:

'The Duke of Strathythan (I am writing of course of the seventeenth Duke, not of his present Grace) was, as everybody knows, famous for his hospitality. It was not perhaps generally known that the Duke was as witty as he was hospitable. I recall a most amusing incident that happened the last time but two that I was staying at Strathythan Towers. As we sat down to lunch (we were a very small and intimate party, there being only forty-three of us) the Duke, who was at the head of the table, looked up from the roast of beef that he was carving, and running his eye about the guests was heard to murmur, 'I'm afraid there isn't enough beef to go round.'

'There was nothing to do, of course, but to roar with laughter and the incident passed off with perfect savoir faire.'

Just to show you that he's got it right, here are three

extracts from the reminiscences of a real duke, *Men, Women and Things*, by the sixth Duke of Portland, published in 1937:

Lord Lathom had a fine, long beard, and was a man of extremely dignified figure and appearance. Before his creation as Earl of Lathom in 1880, he had for many years, as Lord Skelmersdale, been an effective and popular whip to the Conservative Party in the House of Commons . . . When I knew him, he was still known to his older friends as 'Skelmy'. He was one of the best gun shots of his time; and, when shooting, he divided his beard into two plaits, which he tied behind his neck, out of the way of the stock of his gun. I have never seen this done by anyone else.

I don't suppose anyone else had either. And again:

Lord Colville wore a little gold ball attached to his watch-chain. My wife was very curious as to what it contained, but he made rather a mystery of it, and refused to tell her. At last, after much teasing, he opened it – and she saw a beautiful blue eye! 'I lost one of my eyes in a shooting accident,' he told her, 'and this is a spare one I use when the one I am wearing grows hot and uncomfortable. I have another at home, with a merry twinkle in it; I shall certainly wear that when I have the pleasure of seeing you again.'

And a third from the same source:

On another occasion when King Edward honoured us with his presence, he was suffering from a rather serious injury to one of his feet. His Majesty therefore shot from a bath chair. At one of the rises where the pheasants flew very high, Lord Ripon killed a particularly high-flying bird stone dead, when, to everyone's dismay, it seemed about to fall on H. M.'s head. Fortunately it fell a few inches wide, but hit the arm of the bath chair, burst open, and covered the King with blood and feathers. Naturally, H. M. was none too pleased, but after the mess had been cleaned up, he simply laughed and made a joke of it.

The Duke of Portland was not, of course, as good a writer as Leacock. But Leacock faithfully reproduces the spirit of trivia portentously presented, and the wide-eyed certainty that the minutiae of upper-class existence are not only worth recording, but also the laws of the universe. When it comes to plaited beards, detonating pheasants and twinkling false eyes, perhaps they are.

INTRODUCTION

I have categorised these outbreaks of 'the higher lunacy' under various chapter headings. Many of the leading characters make several appearances, and it is sometimes difficult to follow the comings and goings of the *dramatis personae*. This is because, under the impact of marriage and inheritance, their names frequently change. In the words of Hilaire Belloc: 'Lord Lucky by a curious fluke/Became a most important Duke'. This seems to happen to quite a few of them. I will provide what signposts I can, but we are dealing with profound mysteries, and to understand the whole thing properly you need to be the sort of person who knows that the name 'Bertie' is pronounced 'Bartie', 'Ralph', 'Rayf', and that the word 'lunch' absolutely does not exist, except perhaps as a verb.

*

Any anthology of sayings and quotations depends ultimately on hearsay. However well-attested an anecdote may be, at some point it has been retailed by word of mouth, and thereafter repeatedly. Many of the stories in this book appear elsewhere in varied forms, sometimes attributed to other actors and speakers. Stories that start out as genuine are 'improved' and embroidered by any who think they can do better, and their version becomes the most repeated one. There is no guarantee of authenticity. I have not actually invented anything – at least I don't think so – but I have frequently depended on my memory. I have spread my net as widely as possible, and I have not shunned stories that show the subjects of this book in a very bad light. But I have avoided some themes: serious crime, for instance, likewise misers. Misers are unquestionably eccentrics, but their stories are so miserable and in some way degraded that I have not dealt with them.

To look at the funny side of people's conduct carries with it the risk of bias. It is easy to make them look solely ridiculous, as if they had no other facets to their characters. Lord Durham, for instance, whom I quote as saying that a man can 'jog along' on £40,000 a year (approximately £1,700,000 in modern terms), was also 'Radical Jack', a distinguished statesman and colonial administrator, credited with endowing Canada with representative government. And the tenth Duke of Hamilton, who appears in these pages because of his unfortunate burial, was, for all his peculiarities, an effective ambassador to Russia on a 'special mission' in 1807, during the Napoleonic Wars, which cannot have been an easy post. The bias can also work the other way. Humour is sympathetic, and to present someone in a comic light may mask other truly scaly behaviour. In my view, compared with other commentators, I have, in the interests of light relief, gone very easy on Bendor, second Duke of Westminster. On the whole I have tried to present the subjects of this book as eccentric – a quality I greatly admire. I quote the *Shorter Oxford English Dictionary*:

> *Eccentricity*: 1. The quality of being abnormally centred... of not having the axis in the centre . . . 4. The quality or habit of deviating from what is customary; irregularity, oddity, whimsicality.

Perfectly put. How many, in the following pages, have their axis somewhere other than in the centre?

'At Stirling, in the middle
of the night, I milked
the goat in the first-class
waiting room which I should
not have done as I only had
a third-class ticket.'

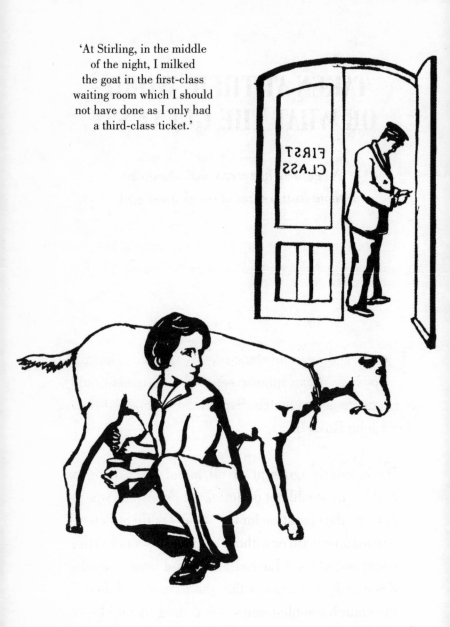

TAKEN AT THEIR WORD, OR WHAT THE GREAT SAY

'No garden, however small, should be without its two acres of rough woodland.'

Privileged circumstances give their fortunate possessors an infinite sense of entitlement, and a self-confidence to match. Sydney Smith noticed this in Lord John Russell:

He is utterly ignorant of all moral fear; there is nothing he would not undertake. I believe he would perform the operation for the stone – build St Peter's – or assume (with or without ten minutes' notice) the command of the Channel Fleet: and no one would discover by his manner that the patient had died – the church tumbled down – and the Channel Fleet been knocked to atoms.

This chapter deals with the ways in which the great unconsciously betray their sense of entitlement and privilege. This can take the form of a sort of fretful innocence, expressing a detachment from day-to-day practicalities that doesn't matter because there is always someone else there to see to them. It can take other forms too, and these we shall encounter later. At some moment during the First World War, the Duke of Northumberland hauled at a bell pull in Alnwick Castle to summon tea. Some miles away the bell rang in the butler's pantry, and the procession set out – the butler in the lead, one footman pushing the trolley and a second footman bearing other essentials like an additional supply of hot water. Under the butler's supervision the two footmen laid out the tea service and stood back. The Duke looked on, pained.

'Snelgrove,' he said, or it may have been Bladesmith or Perkins or whatever the butler's name was. 'How is it that you have not brought us any cucumber sandwiches?'

'I regret to inform your grace that as a result of wartime restrictions there is no bread.'

The Duke pondered this for a moment.

'Then why the deuce haven't you brought us toast?'

Another duke displayed almost equal detachment from real life. One of the Dukes of Devonshire, possibly the seventh or eighth (some say, however, that it was the first Duke of Westminster), was one day buying

16

silver at Asprey, when he noticed some circular silver rings. He turned to his steward and enquired of him what they were.

'Those, your Grace, are napkin rings'.

'A napkin ring?'

'Your Grace, when the middle classes breakfast, they take a fresh napkin, and when they have finished, they fold it, and roll it and place it through the ring. They use it again for luncheon, tea, and dinner. Only at the end of the day is it sent to be laundered.'

The Duke was shocked. 'They use the same napkin throughout the day?'

'They do, Your Grace.'

'My goodness,' said the Duke, 'I had no idea such poverty existed'.

These stories do not have to be true. They are perfect as parables. Imagine being so cushioned by your circumstances that you are completely unaware of the connection between bread and toast, or of the notion that napkins might be used more than once between launderings. It is a window into another mental world – one that might have been invented by P. G. Wodehouse, but was in fact enlarged and elaborated by him to create a sort of Garden of Eden of deranged and disordered minds. A similar story is told of the heir to the ninth Duke of Marlborough who complained that his toothbrush wouldn't foam.

Hitherto it had been his valet's job to apply toothpaste to brush, and the young gentleman knew nothing of such technicalities.

A similar technophobia can be found in Osborne de Vere Beauclerk, twelfth Duke of St Albans (1874–1964). Familiarly known as 'Obby', the Duke was averse to any small chore involving practical aptitude or dexterity. He used to entreat the porter at Brooks's Club: 'Wind my watch for me, there's a good fellow.' (He may be the source of an anonymous story concerning a man about town to whom it was pointed out that his watch had stopped. 'Impossible,' he replied, 'my valet winds it every morning.)

Examples of such extreme innocence and incompetence are rare, but very often, in a smaller way, the privileged betray their inner mental world in what they say – and, at the same time, are frequently both designedly and accidentally funny. 'Debo' Mitford (1920–2014), Nancy Mitford's youngest sister, married the eleventh Duke of Devonshire, thereby becoming the chatelaine of Chatsworth House with its 297 rooms, 53 lavatories, and 7,873 panes of glass. When asked what it was like to live there she answered: 'Well, it's no place to house train a puppy.'

She was devoted to goats, and travelling once from Scotland to England with her goat she was overtaken by a crisis: 'At Stirling, in the middle of the night, I milked the goat in the first-class waiting room which I should not have done as I only had a third-class ticket.'

(Her grandmother held the firm belief that only severe concussion would get rid of woodworm in furniture. She carried with her a little mallet, and thwacked the chairs and tables as she went about her house.)

The Duchess was also a source of remarks in others. When she was thirty-four, and an acknowledged beauty, Lucian Freud – never one to flatter his sitters – painted her. When the painting was exhibited a woman was overheard to say. 'That's the Dowager Duchess. It was done a year before she died.' Another viewer asked 'Who is that?' Being nearby the Duke replied, 'It's my wife.' 'Well, thank God it isn't mine.'

She was, however, too down to earth to be the unnamed peeress who was told that there was dry rot in the west wing of her husband's country house and replied: 'Doesn't everybody have dry rot in the west wing?'

And here is a very barbed remark, perhaps not unconscious, from Nancy Mitford, revealing a whole world of privilege waiting in the background: 'I love children, especially when they cry, for then someone takes them away.'

Even in the highest offices of state this distant and detached view of reality is evident. During his stint as Chancellor of the Exchequer, Lord Randolph Churchill (1849–94), father of Winston Churchill, had the decimal system explained to him by a mathematically minded friend. A great light dawned.

'I never could make out what those damned dots meant,' he exclaimed.

Just such an awakening was in store for Emily Mary, first Marchioness of Salisbury (1750–1835). Many facets of her behaviour scandalised society – gambling, extravagance, but worst of all cutting church services and in general having little time for religion. She was so ill-acquainted with the Scriptures that the full story of Genesis came as a terrible shock to her. Told that Adam, when caught out by God eating the forbidden fruit, had cravenly blamed it on Eve, her indignation knew no bounds: 'A shabby fellow indeed!'

(The spirited Marchioness died horribly. Rising from the table, her towering eighteenth-century hair-do got entangled in a chandelier. Her headdress burned, the Marchioness burned, and eventually the whole house was destroyed.)

Unreality about money was the downfall of many a noble house. Quite apart from obviously disastrous behaviour, like gambling, and massively extravagant spending on activities like building palaces, breeding race horses, shooting and many another ruinous whim, the sheer scale of aristocratic living reduced many a peer to sorrowful contemplation of his finances.

When John Lambton, first Earl of Durham (1792–

1840) remarked that '£40,000 a year is a moderate income – such as one man might jog along with,' he was not speaking from experience, his own income being a healthy £80,000 a year at the time – or between £6m and £8m in modern money.

Less complacent was Richard Plantagenet Campbell Temple-Nugent-Brydges-Chandos-Grenville, third Duke of Buckingham and Chandos (1823–89). Inheriting huge debts from his father, and struggling with the expenses of an active public career, he was subject to repeated financial crises. During one of these the auditors tentatively suggested that perhaps six chefs was excessive, and one, the pastry cook, might possibly be dispensed with. The Duke gazed bleakly at his straitened future. 'Can't a chap have a biscuit?' he complained.

Before we leave the theme of unreflective innocence, aka stark ignorance, I must desert the aristocracy, and the upper class and, indeed, any known class, upper or otherwise, to include a remark by Sam Goldwyn. Informed that he could not film *The Well of Loneliness* by Radclyffe Hall because it was about lesbians, he dismissed quibbles of this kind with an expansive wave of his cigar.

'So,' he said impatiently, 'make them Latvians!'

It goes without saying that the upper classes have always had a nice line in put-downs. The men, in particular, with their Corinthian upbringing and their *nil admirari* airs and graces, have always been in a strong position to deliver cutting rebukes. And their women have never been far behind. But it is not always necessary to be cruel to put someone in their place.

Henry Charles Brougham, third Baron Brougham and Vaux (1836–1927) – or it may have been the fourth Baron; the sources conflict – gave a luncheon party. The guest of honour, a famous society beauty, arrived shockingly late.

'Sorry, dahlings,' she breathed, 'I saw this absolutely *exquisite* little chandelier, and I simply *had* to buy it.'

Lord Brougham looked straight ahead and said quietly:

'I once knew a man who bought a chandelier *after* luncheon.'

I don't suppose she even noticed, or would have understood if she had. But in less kindly hands silken words can cut deeper than the most violent abuse.

When, as a young man, Constant Lambert (1905–51), the British composer and conductor, met the writer and critic Lytton Strachey, he reminded Strachey that they had met before, four years previously.

'You don't remember me, Mr Strachey? We met four years ago.'

'Quite a nice interval, I think. Don't you?' remarked Strachey, and passed on.

(Strachey was an unashamed homosexual and also a pacifist. When brought before a tribunal in the First War he was asked by the examining officer: 'So you say you're a pacifist. Well, what would you do if you saw a Hun soldier ravishing your sister?'

Strachey famously replied: 'I would try to interpose my body.')

The film director Sir Alfred Hitchcock (1889–1980) had a similar gift of telling repartee, and was also wedded to the pleasures of the table. Dining one evening with new acquaintances, he was disappointed by the scanty fare provided. At the end of the meal his host said: 'I do hope you will dine with us again soon.'

'By all means,' said Hitchcock. 'Let's start now.'

And the perils of the dinner table bring us to F. E. Smith (1872–1930), later the first Earl of Birkenhead. This powerful figure was bound to make his way into these pages sooner or later, because his gift of vituperative wit has never been equalled. Most of his repertoire belongs to the chapter on the judiciary, but two general ones, not very vituperative, are relevant here. On one occasion a lady seated next to him at a dinner party subjected him to a long harangue about her dietary preferences, mainly based on squeamishness. She concluded: 'And Mr Smith. I could never eat tongue because it comes from an animal's mouth!'

'Try an egg,' he suggested.

Smith was given to dropping into the Athenaeum Club, of which he was not a member, to relieve himself as he walked to the House of Lords. In due course the porter plucked up the courage to ask: 'Excuse me, sir. Are you a member?'

'Good Lord,' said Smith. 'You don't mean this is a club as well?' (The Athenaeum occupies a position of the utmost grandeur at the corner of Pall Mall and Waterloo Place. Another version gives his reply as 'There's more to me than that, my man!')

Smith did not always get away with it unchallenged. Margot Asquith (1864–1945), wife of the Prime Minister Herbert Asquith and herself a very fertile source of quotations and put-downs, said of Smith, 'Lord Birkenhead is very clever, but sometimes his brains go to his head.' There is nothing in the surrounding context to tell us whether she meant this as a witticism, or whether it was just clumsy phrasing. Nor do the rest of her quoted *bon mots* give us much clue. Here they are – some of them:

'Lloyd George? There is no Lloyd George. There is a marvellous brain; but if you were to shut him in a room and look through the keyhole there would be nobody there.'

'She tells enough white lies to ice a wedding cake.' (Speaking of Lady Desborough, society beauty, hostess, leading light of The Souls [see below], and mistress to a string of younger lovers.)

Her most famous put-down is, alas, probably apocryphal. Meeting Margot Asquith for the first time, the platinum-blonde Hollywood star, Jean Harlow, made the mistake of calling her by her Christian name. She made the further error of pronouncing it to rhyme with 'got'. Asquith looked at her witheringly and said:

'The "T" is silent, as in Harlow.' (It is sometimes said to have been the actress Margot Grahame who delivered this famous rebuke.)

(Margot Asquith was a prominent member of The Souls, a group of serious-minded young socialites that gathered round the figure of Violet Manners, Duchess of Rutland, and spoke much of their souls. They were so studiedly high-minded that an anonymous wit was moved to write: *Said the Duchess of Rutland at tea/ 'My boy, do you fart when you pee?'/I replied with some wit/ 'Do you belch when you shit?'/I felt that was one up to me.*)

Lady Asquith was on familiar and easy terms with the dead, whom she frequently consulted. Speaking to Lord David Cecil, she confided that she had a very low opinion of the late King's doctor, a man called Lord Dawson. 'He was not a good doctor. King George himself told me he would never have died had he had another doctor.' (As it happened she was not entirely wrong: Lord Dawson of Penn admitted in his diary, which was released in 1986, that he had hastened the dying king's demise by injecting him with morphine followed by cocaine, in order that the death should be announced in the following morning's edition of *The Times* 'rather than the less appropriate evening journals'.)

But the dead did not always meet with her favour: 'I always knew the living talked rot, but it's nothing to the rot the dead talk.'

A put-down, ideally, should be delivered face-to-face, but I think it counts if the victim merely hears the insult. At the Congress of Vienna that great deliverer of cutting remarks, the Duke of Wellington, found himself confronted by a group of embittered French officers. They showed their resentment by silently turning their backs on him. A female bystander attempted to apologise to the Duke for this rudeness, but he cut her short with perhaps the most blistering remark ever addressed by one soldier to another, albeit indirectly.

'I have seen their backs before, Madam,' he said.

And of course there is his most famous put-down of all. George Jones, a painter of military scenes, had the mixed fortune to bear a striking resemblance to the hero of Waterloo – nose and all. The Duke was accosted in the street one day by a gentleman who was deceived by this resemblance.

'Mr Jones, I believe,' he said.

'If you believe that, you'll believe anything,' answered the Duke.

Put-downs certainly reflect arrogance and self-certainty, and this is to be expected in those born with very large silver spoons in their mouths, or in people who have risen in the world of practical affairs. But it is distressing to record that the intelligentsia – or at least that segment of it that intersects with the upper class – are equally capable of blinding unconcern for their victim's feelings.

Inevitably, the novelist Evelyn Waugh heads this list. Here he is on the subject of Stephen Spender, the poet: 'To see him fumbling with our rich and delicate language is to experience all the horror of seeing a Sèvres vase in the hands of a chimpanzee.'

And even more vituperatively on the subject of his friend, Randolph Churchill, after Churchill's operation to have a non-malignant tumour removed: 'How typical of modern science to find the only part of Randolph that was not malignant and remove it.'

The writer Somerset Maugham achieved such immense popular success that some elements of the press compared him with Shakespeare – a comparison he was not very quick to disclaim. He received this caution from his brother, Viscount Maugham, a successful lawyer: 'Dear Willie, you may well be right in thinking you write like Shakespeare . . . One word of brotherly advice. *Do not attempt the sonnets!*'

Intellectuals are especially hard on each other. This

is Edith Sitwell on Virginia Woolf: 'I enjoyed talking to her, but I thought *nothing* of her writing. I considered her "a beautiful little knitter".'

And a very *de haut en bas* contribution from Lord Byron: 'In general I do not draw well with literary men – not that I dislike them but – I never know what to say to them after I have praised their last publication.'

And not only writers. Philosophers can fall out even more drastically. Bertrand Russell (the third Earl Russell) and Ludwig Wittgenstein notoriously disagreed at their first meetings: 'My German engineer, I think, is a fool. He thinks nothing empirical is Knowable – I asked him to admit that there was not a rhinoceros in the room, but he wouldn't.'

Russell gave another account in which it was a hippopotamus. They were in a lecture room at the time, and Russell went to the lengths of looking under all the desks to disprove the presence of a pachyderm, but without convincing Wittgenstein. I ask you to picture this incident. Here are the two fathers of analytical philosophy – two names that would certainly be near the top if you were asked to compile a list of the Great Minds of the Twentieth Century, crawling about the floor of a Cambridge lecture room, looking for a hippo, or, as it may be, a rhino.

Such is the life of the mind.

They had obviously never read Dr Johnson. The

Doctor was challenged to refute the idea that he could not prove the existence of a chair in the room when his back was turned to it and he could not see it. He raised his foot and kicked vigorously backwards, knocking the chair over. 'I refute it thus!' he declared. (In fairness I must add that Russell came to regard Wittgenstein as a genius, and the two men were an important influence on each other.)

Whether the pachyderm in question may be identified as a hippo or a rhino is of little importance as it did not exist – a more pressing need for Bertrand Russell was to clarify his own identity after he and another Lord Russell were taken for each other on a number of occasions. Finally, in 1959, he and the lawyer, soldier and historian Lord Russell of Liverpool wrote a joint letter to *The Times*:

> Sir,
> In order to discourage confusions which have been constantly occurring, we beg herewith to state that neither of us is the other.
> Yours, etc.,
> Russell (Bertrand, Earl Russell)
> Russell of Liverpool (Lord Russell of Liverpool.

Philosophers can sometimes find themselves way outside their comfort zone, but let it never be said they lose their nerve. The British philosopher A. J. Ayer found himself at a party in New York. Seeing an exceptionally good-looking girl, he went over to talk to her. She was Naomi Campbell, and she was already talking to a dauntingly large man of African-American ancestry. He took umbrage at Ayer's intervention:

'Do you know who the fuck I am? I'm Mike Tyson, the heavyweight champion of the world.'

'And I am the former Wykeham Professor of Logic. We are both pre-eminent in our field. I suggest we talk about this like rational men,' replied Ayer, opting decisively for his own field.

We have wandered from the theme of accidental self-revelation, and, of course, self-revelation is often deliberate, since those who truly love themselves can dwell lovingly even on their faults, especially if it involves making a joke.

'I have taken more out of alcohol than alcohol has taken out of me.' Sir Winston Churchill.

Lord Castlerosse – variously estimated as weighing between 18 and 22 stone – made a similar reference to himself while playing golf with Nancy Cunard.

'What's your handicap,' she asked.

'Drink and debauchery,' replied Castlerosse. And when criticised by his uncle and employer, Lord Revelstoke, for invariably arriving late for work he pointed out: 'But look how early I go.

The last two examples in this chapter take us back to our starting point; privileged circumstances, a sense of entitlement and corresponding self-confidence. The first is an example of conscious arrogance, maliciously deployed. The second an example of amiable and entirely unconscious superiority.

First the dandy – Beau Brummell. Best known for his question 'Who's your fat friend?' addressed to Lord Alvanley who was in the company of the Prince Regent at the time. Brummell was often less sympathetic than this suggests, and affected an airy snobbery that was perhaps a defence against his own comparatively humble origins. His pose was that of the bored exquisite, and nothing bored him more than romantic raptures, fashionable at the time, about travel and scenery. Asked by a visitor, who had been very long-winded in his praise of the English Lake District, which of the lakes he preferred, Brummell turned with an exhausted sigh to his valet:

'Robinson.'
'Sir.'
'Which of the Lakes do I admire?'
'Windermere, sir.'
'Ah, yes – so it is. Windermere, to be sure.'

The story is also told of two bluestocking women

tackling Brummell on the similar subject of the Italian Lakes. There are echoes of Pitt the Younger who used to humiliate his political colleagues by keeping a young scholar of Westminster School to answer his questions when his colleagues could not.

Lastly to the more agreeable figure of the naturalist and collector, Walter, the second Baron Rothschild. Born to vast wealth, Rothschild was able to pursue his passion for natural history. In the manner of the time this involved a good deal of killing and stuffing, and eventually his collection amounted to over 300,000 specimens. It is known that he drove carriages drawn by zebras at the start of the twentieth century – photographs exist – and there is a picture of him riding a giant tortoise. (The shoemaker John Lobb's is said to have used a zebra-drawn cart in the 1930s – *see* p. 52; but *see also* Afterword, pp. 207–8.)

In addition to natural history, he was a great gardener, and his gardens at Tring were so important that he used to be invited to lecture to horticultural associations and other bodies.

He was once asked to address the horticultural society of a large northern town. The members of this group were men who had a small front garden dedicated to flowers, and a back garden given over to a pigeon loft, and possibly a kennel for the whippets. But they took their gardening seriously. Lord Rothschild opened his address with this helpful advice: 'No garden, *however small*, should be without its two acres of rough woodland.'

'Standing on the pavement
between Fortnum & Mason and
Hatchards, he shot them both
dead as they made their way down
Piccadilly – a very tricky left
and right.'

PLAY UP! PLAY UP!
AND PLAY THE GAME!

'J'adore ce cricket; c'est tellement Anglais!'

In no area has the British establishment shown so much enthusiasm as in sport. Strictly, 'sport' refers only to engagements with nature – like mountaineering and the hunting sports – in which there is no agreed method of 'winning', and which are pursued for the love of the activity and not necessarily to 'win' in some way. Engagements with other people, in competition with them, with the aim of winning – by scoring points, or by measuring time or distance – are 'games'. Games are competitive; sports are not. The best sports involve personal risk. These can never be hard and fast distinctions. There are too many borderline examples. Skiing, for instance, is unmistakably an engagement with nature, but also often competitive. Also horse racing, yachting, even motor racing, and many others.

But the distinction is useful because it highlights another aspect of 'sport' – it carries strong ethical overtones, best summed up as 'magnanimity in victory, grace in defeat, generous conduct, and fair play'. No activity that involves 'sledging', ball-tampering and match fixing (cricket), or the hysterics of association football, or doping, or any of the many other abuses of professional, competitive games, deserves to be called a 'sport'. Nor can its practitioners be called 'sportsmen'.

The matter of 'games' can best be left to Sarah Bernhardt. The great actress was performing at Manchester, and diverted herself by taking a drive in the surrounding countryside in an open car. Attracted by shouts she found herself watching a game of football. The ground was wet; the contestants were covered in mud. Bernhardt, clad in white fur, and dripping jewellery, stood up and watched the game enthralled. When it was over, she sank back into her seat and said: *'J'adore ce cricket; c'est tellement Anglais!'*

The British upper crust has pursued sports and games alike with manic zeal, and not always in a sportsmanlike manner. But most of all they pursued the field sports – hunting, shooting and fishing. Among their practitioners the field sports have often assumed the status of a religion. In late 1914, when all his hunt servants had enlisted in the forces, an unnamed Master of Hounds was compelled to hunt his hounds himself. Hounds were hot on the scent of a fox when it cleverly decided to run across a pitch where two teams were playing football, thereby confusing the scent. The MFH sat his horse in silence as his hounds cast about. He glared with undisguised disapproval at the football players. Eventually he spoke.

'Good God!' he said. 'What the devil do you men think you're doing? *Don't you realise there's a war on?'*

Curiously, hunting, though by far the most important of the field sports in the context of this book, does not yield many incidents of the higher lunacy. It does not need to. The entire process is a wholescale exercise in applied lunacy that subsumes any lesser outbreaks. As the great Dr Johnson might have remarked: 'What man would get on a horse who has the wit to walk? For what is a horse, but a machine for throwing you to the ground and rolling on you?'

Astonishing numbers of people continue to ride horses even when there are preferable alternatives. And it is often the launching pad of further outbreaks of madness. The Hon. Mrs Victor Bruce, throughout the 1920s and 30s, set numerous speed and distance records in cars, powerboats and aircraft. She was the first woman to be fined for speeding (1919; the first of many such convictions). She came sixth overall in the 1927 Monte

Carlo rally having driven 1,700 miles in 72 hours without sleeping. In 1929 she captured the world single-handed record by driving for 24 hours at an average speed of 89 mph. She went on to drive a power boat from Dover to Calais and back in 1hour 47minutes. And in July 1930 she bought an aeroplane, learnt to fly, and in September set off on the first successful solo circumnavigation of the world by air. She dispensed with a parachute to save weight, and crashed in the Arabian Desert. When flying over Hong Kong she noticed it was 11 November, and at 1100 hours she turned off her engine to observe the two-minute silence. These, and many other achievements, nearly always involved a speed record of some kind. Mildred Mary Bruce loved speed.

'Speed,' she said, 'has always fascinated me since my first pony bolted.'

It is sad to record that they simply don't make ponies like that any more.

Horses continue to preoccupy the upper classes. On one occasion Mrs Thatcher found herself without the required majority for a vote in the House of Lords. She upbraided the Government Chief Whip in the House of Lords, Lord Denham.

'I do not create peers to have them vote against me in the House of Lords.'

For once, someone stood up to her.

'Prime Minister,' retorted Lord Denham. 'Even you

should know better than to expect me to find you a majority during Gold Cup week.'

By those who love them, horses are never forgotten. My parents spent their twilight years in a manor house converted into an old people's home. One of their fellow inmates was a retired brigadier of Indian cavalry. He was extremely tall and lean. His long legs were slightly bowed from years in the saddle. His piercing, pale blue eyes had the faraway look of one who has long ago decided to live elsewhere. Age had made him very insecure on his slightly bowed pins. One day he rose from the luncheon table and headed for the door. Immediately he was intercepted by one of the nursing staff.

'Brigadier. Where are you going?'

'To my room.'

'But you can't go to your room unaided, Brigadier. It's too far.'

He glared at her with hot impatience.

'Then get my horse,' he snapped.

Fishing we may pass over. Without doubt a manifestation of insanity, it is too solitary to generate much in the way of observed lunacy. ('Fishing is unquestionably a form of madness, but, happily for the once-bitten, there is no cure.' Lord Home, aka Alec Douglas-Home.) There is perhaps one outbreak we should record, which may be apocryphal. Certainly I have it only by hearsay. The late

Lord Mountbatten was once fishing for salmon on the River Dee in Scotland. He was successful, and hooked a salmon. He had chosen to fish without a ghillie, and as he drew the fish towards the bank he attempted to gaff it. He was watched from afar by Prince Philip who could not understand the difficulty Mountbatten appeared to be having. As he drew closer he spotted the problem.

'Take the bloody cork off the end,' he shouted.

We must pass on to shooting, and here we hit pay dirt. There is something about the clean reek of cordite that – well, you will see what it does.

We shall start at the top. On 18 December 1913, at Hall Barn in Buckinghamshire, King George V, the Prince of Wales, their host Lord Burnham, Lord Bertie Vane Tempest, the Honourable Harry Stonor, Lord Dalhousie, Lord Charles Fitzmaurice and Lord Ilchester killed 3,937 pheasants – a record that still stands, as well it might. Consider for a moment the logistics of this. The King and his son were both very good shots, and Harry Stonor one of the best in the country. But the national average of marksmanship sticks obstinately at one successful shot in three. To kill almost 4,000 pheasants, you would therefore require close on 12,000 cartridges. The standard load for a 12-bore cartridge is 30 grams, so provision would have to be made for the transport and distribution of 360 kilograms of lead. A small army of pickers-up with dogs would be needed to retrieve the dead and wounded. And the guns, supported by loaders, would have to be firing almost continuously to achieve such a score in the daylight hours. It can scarcely be described as a sport. Small wonder that during their return journey to London, the King remarked to his son.

'I shouldn't say anything about this if I were you. I think we may have overdone it today.'

(There is a rival claim. On 5 December 1909, 3,824 pheasants, 15 partridge, 526 hares, 92 rabbits and 3 various were shot at Warter Priory in Yorkshire. A bigger total bag, but not the record for pheasants.)

The 'Hall Barn Incident' was merely the culmination of a trend in game shooting that began with the advent of the breech-loading gun in the mid-nineteenth century. It was a time of agricultural depression in Britain, and besides, farming methods were reasonably 'game friendly'. Land owners with deep enough pockets could therefore devote their estates to cultivating game for shooting – and they did. The record bags of other birds were equally impressive: 1,671 partridges at Holkham, Norfolk; 2,929 grouse at Littledale in Lancashire; and a stunning 6,943 rabbits at Blenheim, Oxfordshire. These are all bags shot in one day by a team of guns.

I must add a personal reminiscence about rabbits. The late Mrs Betty McKeever, at one time my employer, claimed to hold the record of rabbits shot by one gun in a day. Her family owned a property in Scotland where there was a disused railway cutting, much colonised by rabbits. Sometime in the 1920s she instructed the keepers, helped by the entire staff of the estate, indoor and outdoor, to spend the night blocking up the rabbit holes in the sides of the cutting. When dawn broke Mrs McKeever was to be found at one end of the cutting, armed with three shotguns, and supported by two loaders. The keepers began to beat the cutting towards her. There were prodigious numbers of rabbits. Betty McKeever fired, fired again, and kept on firing. By the time the keepers had beaten out the whole length of the cutting, Mrs McKeever stood triumphant, wreathed in powder smoke, and surrounded by 729 dead rabbits.

She was but a slip of a girl at the time. She was given a pack of hounds (the Blean Beagles) as a ninth birthday present, and she died at eighty-nine, having been a Master of Hounds for eighty years. Her nearest and dearest were disconcerted, on opening her will, to find that she had left her body to be fed to the hounds.

Other 'one-day' bags to individual guns include 780 partridges to Maharajah Duleep Singh, and 1,070 grouse to Lord Walsingham.

But statistics cannot convey the utter strangeness of the shooting habits of rich Victorians and Edwardians. To start with they were not very particular about what they shot. Edward VII, visiting Egypt, shot 28 flamingos, and then went on to shoot the bats that infested the tomb of Rameses IV. These proved more testing, and only one succumbed. But at least he shot these targets deliberately. In December 1891, distracted by the ladies to whom he was talking, he shot his own shooting stick to smithereens in mistake for a hare. It needs to be pointed out that he was not sitting on it at the time. And while Lord Hartington certainly intended to shoot dead a pheasant flying low through a gate at Chatsworth in Derbyshire, I don't suppose it was his intention to shoot dead the retriever that was pursuing it, nor to pepper (a) the retriever's owner, and (b) the chef from Chatsworth House who had walked down to watch the shooting. When asked if he regretted taking this risky shot he replied 'Well of course. If I had killed the chef we'd have had no dinner.' This deplorable performance became a matter of merriment, and the spot was thereafter known as 'Harty's Stand'. (Shooting humour does not reach very great heights. A gun who accidentally peppered his father on his father's own grouse moor was known thereafter as 'Baghdad'.)

Titled sportsmen of the nineteenth century seem to have had it in for man's best friend. Shooting at Wynyard, the property of Lord Londonderry, Lord Randolph Churchill, father of Winston Churchill, shot a pet dachshund belonging to a lady spectator, also a cousin of his. (They obviously didn't mind taking low shots in those days.) The lady was greatly distressed, and Lord Randolph, stricken with remorse, took the sad little corpse to London's best taxidermist, had it stuffed and mounted in an appealing posture, and gave it to the grieving lady as a Christmas present. It was not received in the spirit in which it was given.

The Marquess of Ripon, unassailably the best shotgun shot of his age, some would say ever, killed a phenomenal 370,728 head of game in his life, including a left and right at rhinoceroses with a four-bore rifle – a massively heavy weapon, firing a projectile a good deal bigger than a golf ball. Shooting is not supposed to be a competitive sport, but inevitably 'The Big Shots' – as they have been called – did get edgy from time to time, with unfortunate results. Ripon himself was once placed next to a gun who shot birds that would otherwise have gone to him. 'Two can play at that game!' he called out, and nothing survived to pass over the other gun for the rest of the drive.

Worse consequences attended his rivalry with Lord Wemyss on the Duke of Cleveland's grouse moor. Wemyss felt that he was gaining the upper hand when a spillage of black powder set his butt alight. He paid little heed. 'Flaming butts do not matter, but to beat the best game shot in England mattered a great deal.' Driven out of the butt by the flames, Lord Wemyss continued to fire at the grouse in the open. The fire spread in the dry roots of the heather, and it took a fortnight, and the entire local labour force carrying buckets of water up from the valley, to put it out. But it was worth it. Lord Wemyss had won.

Loose black powder was dangerous. Lord Walsingham – another dead-eye dick – was shooting partridges with Ripon when the latter saw a flash, and his neighbour disappeared in a dense pillar of smoke – rather like the scenic effects in a baroque opera. His Lordship and his loader were lightly singed, and about a quarter of an acre of His Lordship's vegetation reduced to ashes. Fresh powder was procured, and the shooting continued.

When not setting fire to shooting butts, Lord Walsingham was a dedicated and knowledgeable naturalist. Between drives he could be seen darting about with his butterfly net, and – mark this – *all the humming birds in the Natural History Museum were shot by Lord Walsingham.*

Because of the danger, taking low shots is now entirely frowned on, and shooting ground game (including dachshunds) forbidden during formal drives. But the spirit of trigger-happiness is not dead, and no one could have accused the seventeenth Viscount Mountgarret of low shooting when, in 1982, he fired both barrels at a hot-air balloon flying over his grouse moor near Appletreewick in Yorkshire.

The yellow-and-blue-striped balloon – a fairly conspicuous object – was owned by the Skipton Building Society. It had 'drifted' over Hardcastle Moor as Mountgarret's party was preparing for a drive. Its pilot, Graham Turnbull, later testified that he was taking two passengers – an aircraft technician and a fish fryer – on a pleasure flight. He added: 'There was quite a few people below with guns. Suddenly shots struck the basket and the balloon itself, and I was covered with lead shot.' A six-foot split was later found in the nylon canopy, as well as twenty holes in the protective cover of the gas burner. The two passengers ducked, but the pilot got a pellet in the neck.

The Viscount, who denied recklessly damaging a hot-air balloon, and acting recklessly in a manner likely to endanger an aircraft, claimed that he had fired warning shots because the balloon was in 'extreme danger' from the guns. The magistrates, however, didn't believe him, found him guilty and fined him £1,000 with £600 costs.

His excuse was indeed pretty thin, and it was widely held in the shooting community at the time that Lord Mountgarret had fired in anger, believing the balloonists to be, not innocent pleasure seekers, but anti-shooting activists bent on disrupting his day's sport. Like all good conspiracy theories this remained untested by evidence, since such facts would be damaging to both sides, and would not therefore be adduced in court. Mr Turnbull was perhaps lucky not to share the fate of the Chatsworth retriever and the Wynyard dachshund. Given the short effective range of a 12-bore game gun, Mr Turnbull must have been very low indeed for a balloon flight.

The Viscount's feat echoes a more fortunate episode in the early history of flight. Lieutenant-General Augustus Pitt-Rivers is justly famous as the father of modern archaeology, bringing scientific rigour to a previously amateur occupation. But he has another claim to fame, some would say more glorious. He was the first man to shoot down an aircraft, and probably the only man to have done so with a 12-bore shotgun. His estates at Rushmore in Dorset were in the area much used by the enthusiasts of early flying machines. Shortly before his death the noise of one of these little string and paper machines so disturbed his peace that he seized his shotgun, stepped out onto his lawn, drew a bead on the offender, and fired. The machine had to make a crash landing in the next field, and the pilot climbed out, uttering threats that eventually came to head in a court appearance. But twelve Dorset men and true, made of sterner stuff than the Yorkshire magistrates, could find nothing wrong with shooting at aircraft, and acquitted him.

(The General died in 1900. The 1890s seem a bit early for aviation in Dorset, and it is possible that this story should be credited to his son, George Pitt-Rivers, the black sheep of the family, who was jailed for pro-Nazi sympathies in the 1940s. I can find no evidence for either version, but I feel that General Pitt-Rivers's descendants will not mind his being crowned with such a distinguished laurel.)

'Renting a moor' or owning a pheasant shoot were potent indicators of class and status. To the lucky few who had such things, it seemed strange that others didn't. The happy proprietor of many thousand acres was once talking to a much younger, much poorer man. Seeking common ground, he asked after his pheasants.

'I'm afraid I don't have any,' replied the young man.

'Then it's your own damn fault. Don't feed 'em properly, I'll be bound.'

Some mention must be made of abroad. At the time of most of the material in this book Britain, famously, occupied one quarter of the habitable globe. (This has always struck me as a curious calculation. Surely to any patriotic Briton of the time, any part of the globe not occupied by Britain would have been deemed uninhabitable? Especially the Continent.) They took their sports with them, and adopted others when they got there. It is difficult to decide whether the wilderness of Africa, and the jungles and deserts of India, stimulated the national tendency to erratic behaviour, or merely sopped it up, like a sponge.

Roualeyn George Gordon-Cumming (1820–66) began his big game hunting career in India in 1838, but it was not until he moved to South Africa in 1843 that he discovered his true métier. The interior of Africa, beyond the confines of the Cape Colony, was at this time unexplored – indeed virtually unvisited. Game abounded in numbers unaffected by the sparse indigenous human population. Gordon-Cumming became a hunter. And how. He chronicled his achievements in his book *Five Years of a Hunter's Life in the Far Interior of South Africa.* Of this volume, received at first with incredulity by stay-at-home critics, David Livingstone, who furnished Gordon-Cumming with most of his native guides, wrote: 'I have no hesitation in saying that Mr Cumming's book conveys a truthful idea of South African hunting.'

In the face of such an authority we are not at liberty to doubt that Gordon-Cumming killed elephants by galloping alongside them on a horse and firing a flintlock pistol into them. (It is sad to record that they don't make horses like *that* any more, either.) I was long ago compelled to sell my copy of *Five Years of a Hunter's Life*, but do I have a memory of a picture not only suggesting that he did this, but also showing that he did it *wearing a kilt* . . . ? I think I do.

Active in the same area, and at the same time, was Captain William Cornwallis Harris, also of the East India Company's army. His book, *The Wild Sports of*

Southern Africa, is 359 pages of unfailing astonishment, and it is impossible to know what to quote:

'Smoking is not a fashionable vice among the Matabele, but all classes are passionately addicted to snuffing.'

'The maneless lion of Guzerat is nothing more than a young lion whose mane has not shot forth; and I give this opinion with less hesitation, having slain the "king of beasts" in every stage from whelphood to imbecility.'

Scarcely the straight bat, shooting imbecilic lions.

'A white turban that I wore round my hunting cap, being dragged off by a projecting bough, was instantly charged by three rhinoceros.'

But the palm must go to Major A. E. Wardrop of the Royal Horse Artillery, author of the irresistible *Modern Pig-Sticking*, published in 1914. It is certainly less daft to chase a boar on horseback than an elephant, but it is daft nonetheless. And the British in India took to it like ducks to water.

'I think there is nothing on earth to beat the desperate excitement of getting on terms with a big fighting pig before he makes his point, and then taking his charges until he drops.'

In this state of desperate excitement, no holds were barred:

Two of us were riding a pig up the main street of Durumgarh. He was just ready for me to spear. I drove my horse forward, thinking, 'I've got you.' But not a bit of it; the pig jinked sharp to the right through the open door of a house and forced his way through the wall. He then turned at bay among some woodstacks in the backyard. I broke my spear in him and my pal did ditto. We had to stay and watch him whilst a native ran to the line for fresh spears. Even then we were lucky to kill him without getting a horse cut, as there was no liberty of manoeuvre in the yard. Meanwhile a native woman, an aged man, and two or three couple of brown babies had come out of the house into the street and set up a terrific wailing. We found a rather nasty cut from the pig on one of the children. However Norman proved equal to the occasion when he arrived with the farrier's box, and a few coppers dried away all tears.

Surely they miss us?

But you did not have to go to the ends of the earth to shoot big game. The eighteenth Lord Dunsany was, among other things – poet, novelist, animal rights campaigner, opponent of tail docking in dogs and President of the West Kent branch of the RSPCA – also an unappeasable hunter of big game. He arrived eighteen months late to take up his position of Professor of Poetry at Athens

University because he had been hunting tigers in India. But to his keen disappointment he had never bagged a zebra. Fate was to be kind to him. In the 1930s the famous John Lobb the Bootmakers in St James's is said to have advertised the shop with a small cart drawn by two zebras – among the very few of these bad-tempered animals to have been 'broken' for human use. They trotted around the West End drawing attention to Mr Lobb's hand-made footwear. Lord Dunsany seized his chance. Standing on the pavement between Fortnum & Mason and Hatchards, he shot them both dead as they made their way down Piccadilly – a very tricky left and right. (*See* Afterword, pp. 207–8.)

Looking back over this chapter one can only marvel at the Kaiser's reckless temerity in picking a fight with people like this.

'He compounded his felony by pulling the tie out at intervals and letting it twang back into place, causing Lady Chetwode to blench each time.'

BIAS AND XENOPHOBIA

'Frogs are slightly better than Huns or Wops,
but abroad is unutterably bloody and
foreigners are fiends.'

P eople reared in privilege for many generations can
only sometimes avoid automatic attitudes
towards the less privileged that vary from the merely
condescending to the downright unpleasant. The
subjects of this book were sadly prone to such lapses,
which mostly fall into three categories: contempt for
foreigners and other races; contempt for the middle
classes and the 'lower orders'; and contempt for women.

The upper classes are not alone in expressing
xenophobia, racialism and anti-feminism, so we shall
start on their own ground – class bias, aka snobbery.
First in to bat is Sir Leo Money (1870–1941). By the
irresistible action of nominative determinism, Money
was an economic theorist. He became an MP and

government adviser and, as an Italian-born émigré, attached perhaps too much status to these achievements. In 1928 he was arrested in Hyde Park for committing an act of indecency with Irene Savidge, a twenty-two-year-old valve tester. He told the police 'I am not the usual riff-raff, I am a man of substance.' He proved this by getting off, with the help of Sir William Joynson-Hicks, the Home Secretary, but he remained discontented that 'a person of position could be charged with such an offence', and prompted an enquiry into the conduct of the police. Sir Leo emerged from it with his class dignity more or less intact, but then rather spoiled the effect by being arrested again, in 1933, for embracing a thirty-year-old shop assistant, Ivy Ruxton, on a train between Dorking and Ewell. He was fined £2.

Aversion to the common herd seems to increase with rank. The sixth Duke of Somerset (1662–1748) was described by the politician and historian Thomas Macaulay as 'a man in whom the pride of birth and rank amounted almost to a disease.' While travelling between his estates, he built special houses, so that he would not have to rub shoulders with the populace in inns. On the same peregrinations, servants went before him to clear commoners from the road, and he invented a sign language to spare himself the pain of actual conversation with his employees. His pride did not stop at class distinctions. He was inordinately vain of his appearance, especially the figure he cut during Court ceremonial, and he disinherited his daughter for sitting down in his presence.

Just as patrician, but far more polite, was the third Marquess of Salisbury (1830–1903). So confident of his own status that he did not bother to dress correctly, he was once arrested on suspicion of being a poacher, and was later evicted from the Monte Carlo casino as a tramp. Neither experience gave him a sense of identity with poachers, tramps, or indeed any member of the lower orders. He thought democracy to be a 'dangerous and irrational creed', and loathed electioneering. In his own words:

Days and weeks of screwed-up smiles and laboured courtesy, the mock geniality, the hearty shake of the filthy hand, the chuckling reply that must be made to the coarse joke, the loathsome, choking compliment that must be paid to the grimy wife and sluttish daughter, the indispensable flattery of the vilest religious prejudices, the wholesome deglutition of hypocritical pledges . . .

He certainly took electioneering seriously. I once stood for Parliament, and I can state with absolute certainty that smiling, courtesy, geniality, hand-shaking, chuckling and compliments never occurred to me, which is perhaps why I lost my deposit instead of getting in and becoming prime minister like Lord Salisbury. His aloofness extended to his own class and its institutions. He once accused the Prime Minister, William Gladstone, of conduct unworthy 'of an attorney'. He was asked to apologise, and did so, saying that he had done a grave disservice to attorneys. He referred to the Order of the Garter, to which both his father and grandfather belonged, as: 'A very useful institution. It fosters a wholesome taste for bright colours, and gives old men who have good legs an excuse for showing them.'

Less ill at ease with the electorate was the fourteenth Earl of Home, later Sir Alec Douglas-Home, later still Lord Home of the Hirsel, although he incurred criticism for being too 'old school' and 'out of touch'. How could this possibly be so? queried his daughter, Lady Caroline Douglas-Home: 'He is used to dealing with estate workers. I cannot see how anyone can say he is out of touch.'

In Britain the matter of class status is confusingly split between birth and money. You can be tremendously posh without much money, and you can have all the money in the world and remain dismayingly un-posh. But money certainly helps, and few noses are raised higher than those pointed at people who lack the right possessions, or who behave in a way that lacks the right style. And the strangest distinctions attract the most searching attention:

'Anyone seen in a bus over the age of thirty has been a failure in life.' Loelia, Duchess of Westminster, wife of the second Duke of Westminster, who once attempted to strangle her. (The only possible excuse for such conduct is that not only did he marry a woman called Loelia, but he also had a sister called Lettice.)

Margot Asquith, born Margot Tennant, and second wife of the Prime Minister, Herbert Asquith, took a similarly lofty line. Referring to Asquith's first wife she said: 'She lived in Hampstead and had no clothes.'

Poor old Hampstead. Despised then; excruciatingly up-market now. By 'no clothes' I take it she meant without the sort of *haut-couture* outfits that Margot herself sported. I mean, even in Hampstead she wouldn't have gone about starkers in those days.

Similarly Alan Clark (1928–99), the Tory MP with a taste for other people's wives and daughters, slightingly remarked of Michael Heseltine 'The sort of man who has to buy his own furniture', presumably implying that you're not OK unless you inherit everything you need to furnish a house. Clark inherited not just the furniture, but a castle to put it in. These goodies were the proceeds of the textile trade, his forebears being half of 'Coats & Clark', haberdashers. (His great-great-great-grandfather invented the cotton spool.) Is this really a sound basis from which to shower others with patrician scorn? *Cotton reels?*

Not that the real patricians need any help in pouring scorn. Lord Hartington, later the eighth Duke of Devonshire, was asked how he would reply to the (then) untrammelled Americanism 'Pleased to meet you!' 'So you damned well should be' was the answer. Lord Glasgow – history does not relate which one – in a fit of pique threw one of the waiters through the window of his club. 'Put him on the bill,' he ordered. Clubs – wittily described as 'like a Duke's house with the Duke lying dead upstairs' – often had spacious bow windows facing St James's or Pall Mall so that members could sit there, and, as one of them put it, 'watch the demmed people getting wet outside'.

Condescension comes naturally to some, and can seem almost like good manners. Lord Hugh Cecil (1869–1956), when Provost of Eton, received a visitor who talked of his own affairs at, perhaps, too great a length. Cecil's manner must have betrayed him, because the visitor said: 'I hope that I am not boring you.'

'Not yet,' said Cecil, amiably.

If you have the right credentials you can condescend upwards as well as down. An Old Etonian, falling into reduced circumstances, was obliged to sell matches in the street. An aspiring socialite, not himself an Etonian, in an attempt to impress his companion, challenged him: 'Why are you wearing an Old Etonian tie?'

'Because I can't afford to buy a new one.'

The memorably named Honourable John Wallop, secretary to the Governor of Tasmania in 1884 made no secret of his feelings about the Tasmanian settlers.

'The people are very kindly and hospitable, but one cannot help feeling that going out is more like attending a series of servants' balls and tenants' entertainments.'

But at least he didn't threaten to marry one. Lady Chetwode, wife of Field Marshal Lord Chetwode, had to explain an important social distinction to her daughter, Penelope, who had announced her intention to marry the poet John Betjeman, whose parents owned a workshop in the Pentonville Road that manufactured household knick-knacks.

'We invite people like that to our houses, but we don't marry them.'

Betjeman got his revenge. He not only married Penelope, but at the wedding reception he wore a made-up bow tie on an elastic band – in those days an unpardonable *faux pas*. He compounded his felony by pulling the tie out at intervals and letting it twang back into place, causing Lady Chetwode to blench each time.

Inescapably we arrive at Lord Curzon. We could not easily avoid him. Curzon was so overpoweringly grand that he felt free to condescend even to the King. Invited

to shoot at Sandringham he remarked to King Edward
VII afterwards:

'Well, Sir, the shooting was not much, but the lunch
was excellent.'

The King was immensely proud of his shooting, and
Curzon was not asked again. But two can play at that
game. As an undergraduate Curzon sought permission
from the Master of Balliol, the famous Benjamin Jowett,
to attend a function in London in honour of the Empress
Augusta of Germany. Jowett's refusal was brief:

'I don't think much of Empresses. Good morning.'

Nothing daunted, Curzon went on to enjoy a career
of unparalleled grandeur. In 1915, touring the British
military zone in France, he saw a company of soldiers
resting, and bathing in a canal. He stopped his car and
gazed. Eventually he picked up the speaking tube that
connected him to his chauffeur and said: 'How is it
that I have never been informed that the lower orders
have such white skins?' (Unless he had a companion, or
unless his chauffeur broke silence, it is difficult to see
how this anecdote got into circulation.)

It is good to record that the 'lower orders' sometimes
got their own back. Sir Ralph Payne-Gallwey, the
sportsman and firearms enthusiast, was once dismayed
to discover that the sherry decanter was only half full,
in spite of the fact that neither he nor his guests had
drunk any. He concluded that the butler was taking

illicit swigs at it, and in a mood of merriment he filled it again by peeing into it. The level continued to fall, so he confronted his butler who admitted that he had been taking two tablespoons a day – 'to put in your soup every evening, sir, as the doctor ordered'.

Before we look at the notorious British aversion to foreigners, here is one who hated more or less everything, and said so, sometimes in outbursts of rage so splenetic that they were known among his friends as 'Duff's veiners' (because his veins stood out).

'I don't like men who live, by choice, out of their own country. I don't like interior decorators. I don't like Germans. I don't like buggers, and I don't like Christian Scientists.' Duff Cooper (1890–1954), Conservative politician, diplomat, author, gambler, womaniser and leader of the pack that harried P. G. Wodehouse for his wartime broadcasts. Also husband of the much more agreeable Lady Diana Cooper, natural daughter of Harry Cust (*see* pp. 126–8) and therefore possibly the natural aunt of Lady Thatcher, the Tory Prime Minister (*see* pp. 127–8.)

Now, to the red meat of this chapter.

'Abroad is bloody' – George VI.

How far was Nancy Mitford aware of this when she gave the line 'abroad is unutterably bloody, and foreigners are fiends' to her character Uncle Matt? Or was she quoting the original for Uncle Matt – her father –

directly? Great minds think alike. It's quite possible that Lord Redesdale and his sovereign arrived separately at the same conclusion. Some foreign royalty and nobility were accepted as guests in the great country houses, and even quite liked, so it is a relief to record that the Kaiser, though a frequent visitor, never really captured the British heart. He quite spoiled Cowes Week for Edward VII, who had hitherto made it the highlight of the summer, by his unsportsmanlike conduct in taking it all seriously, and winning. Though billed by the German press as a good shot, he was not, and some of his entourage were downright dangerous. Nevertheless he shot frequently with Lord Lonsdale at Lowther, and when the First World War broke out Lonsdale came in for some criticism for this friendship.

'Ah well,' he said, 'It only shows how careful one should be about picking up acquaintances abroad.'

The Duke of Wellington felt an aversion even to parts of the British Isles. Infuriated at being referred to as 'Irish' simply because he had been born there (a claim that is still made) he retorted: 'Our Lord was born in a stable, but we do not call him a horse.'

But these attitudes are milk and water compared with the real xenophobes. It is perhaps unfair to describe John Aspinall (1926–2000) – gambling impresario, zoo owner, and friend of Lord Lucan – as a mere xenophobe. The fact is he hated all human beings as the obverse of his love of wild animals – preferably big and dangerous wild animals. Britain, he thought, needed 'a bout of beneficial genocide', and although he did not specify which 'gen' should be 'cided', I think we can guess. Challenged about the high death and injury rate among his zookeepers he said 'I would happily sacrifice the lives of my loved ones if that meant saving an endangered species.' To be fair, he also once offered his own life if he could be certain that two million other human beings would go with him.

James Angus Graham, seventh Duke of Montrose (1907–92), managed to be an extreme racialist without any apparent ill will. He simply had views that one hundred years previously would have been considered quite normal – even perhaps liberal – but which were demonstrably inaccurate and foolish in his own lifetime. As a minister in Ian Smith's UDI Rhodesian government, he gave this judgement in an official report: 'The African is a bright and promising little fellow up to the age of puberty. He then becomes hopelessly inadequate and it is well known that this is due to his almost total obsession with matters of sex.'

He held that the Zimbabwe ruins were too advanced to be the work of Africans, and played a leading role in the Rhodesian rejection of Harold Wilson's mediation aboard HMS *Tiger*. It is said that it took twelve minutes to explain Wilson's proposals to the rest of the Rhodesian delegation, but twelve hours to explain them to the Duke.

Duke or no Duke, Graham and all other reactionaries are put in the shade by Colonel Charles de Laet Waldo Sibthorp (1783–1855), who sets the benchmark for blind xenophobia vigorously expressed. He loathed all foreigners and all foreign influences. This propelled him into an unhappy collision with his sovereign, Queen Victoria, who married a foreigner. How could she? First he opposed paying Prince Albert's travelling expenses when he came to 'woo' Victoria. Albert got his expenses. Next, more successfully, he opposed the proposed allowance of £50,000 a year for Albert, and got it reduced to £30,000, on the grounds that £30,000 was 'quite enough for a foreign prince'. He next opposed Prince Albert's sponsorship of the Great Exhibition as a scheme to 'bring even more of his hypocritical foreigners into the country'. He publicly beseeched God to destroy the Crystal Palace with hailstorms. Disraeli, obedient to the instincts of a lifetime, smarmed his approval of the Crystal Palace: 'that enchanted pile which the sagacious taste and prescient philanthropy of an accomplished and enlightened Prince have raised for the glory of England and the delight of two hemispheres'. The Colonel's reaction was more robust: 'I have never set foot [in it] . . . and nothing would induce me to go within a mile of that obscene and insanitary structure.' He warned: 'Take care of your wives and daughters, take care of your property and your lives!' All four were at risk from the hordes of stiletto-wielding foreigners who would flood in to see the Exhibition 'talking gibberish'. Furthermore the Exhibition would favour the artefacts of foreign craftsmen over those of hard-working British workmen: 'How is a man in this country who is accustomed to eat roast beef and drink strong ale, after the manner of a Christian, to compete with those nasty foreigners who live on brown bread and sauerkraut and who manufacture decanters at sixpence a piece?'

He even regaled the House of Commons with his opinion that Prince Albert was the instigator of a foreign plot to overthrow the Empire. He continued to denounce the Crystal Palace exhibition. It would, he said, enable foreign spies to enter Britain and spy on British defences. But his vision of the Foreign Menace was not confined to the Great Exhibition. He also fulminated against: 'The sums of money carried out of the country by foreign opera dancers and singers. I am sorry to say that the higher classes encourage foreigners, whether of character or not, male or female.'

It goes without saying that the Colonel was also hotly opposed to Catholic emancipation and profoundly anti-Semitic. In this last he was hardly alone. Anti-Semitism in Britain was rarely as acute as in France and Germany. Throughout a large part of the nineteenth century the

Conservative Party was led by Benjamin Disraeli, a man of unmistakably Jewish appearance and name. The writer Hilaire Belloc, who peddled a persistent Catholic-biased version of anti-Semitism, nonetheless included in his novel, *The Postmaster General*, a very kindly and sympathetic portrait of a Jewish man, the victim of anti-Semitic prejudice. However, anti-Semitism in Britain during the period covered by this book was widespread, unthinking and largely automatic.

'The main object of the Right Club was to oppose and expose the activities of Organised Jewry, in the light of the evidence which came into my possession in 1938. Our first objective was to clear the Conservative Party of Jewish influence, and the character of our membership and meetings were strictly in keeping with this objective.'

These are the words of Archibald Ramsay, the only sitting MP to be charged with offences under the Official Secrets Act and to be interned under regulation 18B during the Second World War. Members of the Right Club included William Joyce (later better known as 'Lord Haw-Haw', and hanged for treason), Lord Redesdale, the fifth Duke of Wellington, the Marquess of Graham (same chap as the seventh Duke of Montrose, above), and the Earl of Galloway. (Given his views on 'Huns', it is strange to find Lord Redesdale in this largely pro-German company.)

Not all the members, of course, shared to the full Ramsay's barely sane views, which were devoted to 'exposing and frustrating the Jewish stranglehold on our Nordic realm'. But one did, and here we encounter Hugh Richard Arthur Grosvenor, second Duke of Westminster (1879 –1953), known to his friends – a diminishing band throughout his life – as 'Bendor'. In her book, *The Light of the Common Day*, Lady Diana Cooper describes a lunch with her husband, Duff Cooper, and the Duke of Westminster at the Savoy Grill on 1 September 1939:

> The Duke began by 'abusing the Jewish race', adding his praise for the Germans and 'rejoicing that we were not yet at war'. When he added that Hitler knew after all that we were his best friends, he set off the powder-magazine. 'I hope,' Duff spat, 'that by tomorrow he will know that we are his most implacable and remorseless enemies.' Next day Bendor, telephoning to a friend, said that if there was a war it would be entirely due to the Jews and Duff Cooper.

A milder example is Lord Rosebery, who married Hannah Rothschild, by all accounts an enchanting woman whom he adored, and from whose death he never recovered. Nonetheless, if his in-laws lingered too long over the port, he would rap the table and declare: 'To your tents, O Israel'.

No account of British attitudes to race and foreigners would be complete without some mention of the British Empire. It is perhaps easiest to condense this vast subject by taking as an example the Empire's most vocal advocate, the poet and short-story writer Rudyard Kipling (christened Rudyard, by some accounts, because his parents believed him to have been conceived on the banks of Lake Rudyard, a municipal water supply reservoir in the Midlands).

Kipling has often been charged with racialism, and indeed it is possible to cherry-pick from his collected stories plenty that were unquestionably written in the belief that other peoples were inferior to the British – 'His Chance in Life', 'The Comprehension of Private Copper', 'The Head of the District', among others. But it is equally possible to pick many stories that could not possibly have been written by a man who had anything but sympathy, love and understanding for the Indians and India – 'Without Benefit of Clergy', 'In Flood Time', 'Jews in Sushan', 'At Level Nine', and, of course, his one successful novel, *Kim*. This seems to me a good paradigm of British attitudes as a whole – on the one hand dismissive contempt, and on the other real liking and admiration, often present simultaneously in the same person, as with Kipling.

And what of women?

'The Queen is most anxious to enlist every one who can speak or write to join in checking this mad, wicked folly of "Woman's Rights", with all its attendant horrors, on which her poor feeble sex is bent, forgetting every sense of womanly feeling and propriety.' – Queen Victoria in a letter written in 1870.

Need more be said?

'Almost anything that died tempted his palate . . . Rhinoceros, offered
as an outsize pie to a lecture audience ("like very tough beef").'

UNCONTROLLED ECCENTRICITY

'What! The damn feller made it up?'

This chapter deals with those who have gone far beyond the boundaries of mere oddity, but who do not fit into any category. I have tried to find themes to link one example to another, but the fact is that most of the people dealt with in this chapter stand alone – so egregiously potty that they bear no comparison with anyone – not even with their peers. And peers is often the word.

Let us ease our way into this chapter with a few sympathetic animal fixations. Step forward Hastings William Sackville Russell, twelfth Duke of Bedford (1888–1953), a man of many parts. Accused of being both a fascist and a communist, he did not speak to his father for twenty years. Nor did he trouble to inform his son that he had a grandfather who was a duke, nor that he would in due course be a duke himself. His socialism took the agreeable form of advocating ten seconds' work a day from everyone – enough in his view to provide all our requirements. These lapses may be ascribed to his concentration on higher matters – breeding parrots. And pampering them. He fed them chocolates, and, according to Nancy Mitford, he fed his pet spider on roast beef and Yorkshire pudding. He bred many species of parrot, including the Tahiti Blue Lorikeet and the Ultramarine Lorikeet – both 'firsts' for captive breeding. (I have searched the records in vain for a Norwegian Blue.) He further developed a strain of 'homing' budgerigar – (at least according to William Donaldson in *Brewer's Rogues, Villains and Eccentrics*; frankly, I don't believe a word of it). In 1953 the twelfth Duke was found dead of gunshot wounds on his estate in Devon. The coroner recorded accidental death. Others thought suicide. But those who really knew him felt sure he had shot himself by mistake while aiming at a sparrowhawk that was chasing his budgies. Since the sparrowhawk was left in command of the field, we may assume that at least one of them did not home successfully.

Loving animals is fine, but it helps if they love you back. John Aspinall (*see* pp. 64–5), the gambling impresario, established his zoos at Howletts and Port

Lympne in Kent on the principle of close, loving relationships between keepers and animals. The result – which speaks volumes for the greater intelligence of animals – was three keepers killed by tigers, one crushed by an elephant, while a young boy had his arm torn off by a chimpanzee. Aspinall died in 2000, but, unlike Betty McKeever (*see* pp. 41–2), he did not leave his body to be fed to his animals. Rather a poor show, one feels, but the good news about Aspinall is that much of the money that went to establishing his zoos seems to have been ill-gotten. According to *The Hustlers* by Douglas Thompson, and a Channel 4 documentary, *The Real Casino Royale*, Aspinall's Clermont Club, whose founder members included five dukes, five marquesses, and twenty earls, employed a gambling scam called 'the Big Edge' to swindle his customers. Thus did the bank accounts of the great join the body parts of humble working men to feed Aspinall's Siberian tigers. Only Aspinall himself seems to have made no personal sacrifice.

Aspinall fed tigers. Others have looked to the animal kingdom to feed themselves. The Victorian naturalist Frank Buckland (1826–88) was a successful populariser of natural history and an expert on fish culture and fisheries in general. If his advice on pollution and conservation had been heeded, our fisheries would not be in their present parlous state. But his useful public career was eclipsed by a private and public life of surpassing strangeness. He simply settled down to eat all or part of every animal he encountered.

He was helped by his father, a Canon of Christ Church Cathedral, Oxford, who in the Victorian manner was also a noted naturalist and palaeontologist. It was in the Christ Church deanery that young Frank learnt the delights of mice in batter, squirrel pie, horse's tongue and ostrich. Mice became a particular favourite, and as a schoolboy at Winchester: 'I used to skin the mice, run a bit of stick through them, and roast them in front of a fire. A roast field mouse – not a house mouse – is a splendid *bonne bouche* for a hungry boy; it eats like a lark.'

This is perhaps not unusual for a schoolboy: I can remember eating sparrows myself to eke out the school diet, if diet is not too grandiloquent a term. (A sparrow, I can record, eats like a sparrow.) But Buckland carried the habit into adult life to excess. Beyond excess. Here is a contemporary account of him: 'To a lover of natural history it was a pleasant sight to see him at dinner with a chicken before him . . . and see how, undeterred by foolish prejudices, he devoured the brain.'

Others were less appreciative, especially the father of evolution, Charles Darwin himself: 'Though very good natured, he seemed to me a vulgar and almost coarse man. He was incited more by a craving for notoriety, which sometimes made him act like a buffoon, than by a love of science.'

While at Oxford he kept a number of unusual pets – a chameleon, a jackal, an eagle, and a bear which took part in the life of the university dressed in cap and gown, until formally rusticated by the Dean. Knowing his interest in animals as food, the Surrey Zoological Gardens offered Buckland a dead panther: 'It had, however, been buried a couple of days. I got them to dig it up. *It was not very good.*'

Almost anything that died tempted his palate. Whale ('too strong, even when boiled with charcoal'). Elephant trunk soup ('rubbery'). Rhinoceros, offered as an outsize pie to a lecture audience ('like very tough beef'). Porpoise ('broiled lamp-wick'). A giraffe, accidentally barbecued when the giraffe house caught fire, turned out to have delicate white meat, like veal. Buckland compared it with boa constrictor, which he also deemed to be veal-like.

His zoöphagia took a public turn in 1859 when Richard Owen organised 'The Eland Dinner' at the London Tavern, where leading naturalists gathered to decide whether eland should be added to the national diet. And in 1862 Buckland arranged an inaugural dinner for the Acclimatisation Society at Willis's Rooms, St James's, where a hundred guests sampled Japanese sea slug, kangaroo, guan, curassow and Honduras turkey. The kangaroo, Buckland admitted, 'had gone off a bit, but was not bad for all that'. But he found the dinner lacking, and made plans to include capybara on future menus.

Buckland put his expertise in the taste and appearance of dead animals to good account. Visiting the shrine of St Rosalia in Palermo, he pronounced, of her sacred relics, 'Those are the bones of a goat!' He was evicted by the scandalised priests. Shown the 'blood of a martyr' on a cathedral floor, he stooped down, dipped his finger in the blood, tasted it and said, 'Bat's urine!'

Public duties in no wise interfered with his domestic responsibilities. In 1860 he installed his wife, Hannah, in 37 Albany Street, London. With her he also installed monkeys, a jaguar, a donkey, tame mice, cats – and a parrot trained to call for cabs from the window. And these were just the living denizens of number 37. Less fortunate fauna were to be found in the kitchen – stewed moles; dead crocodiles awaiting rendering into stock; porpoise heads, and, of course, plenty of mice. And not only in the kitchen. Buckland's young niece, descending the stairs at Number 37 in the dark, stumbled over a large, soft object, and fell down several flights. She was still more shaken when she discovered the obstacle to be a dead hippopotamus. She was rebuked by her uncle: 'Do be more careful. Hippopotamuses don't grow on trees, you know.'

It is a pleasure to turn to someone whose interest in

animals was less culinary. Charles Waterton (1782–1865) loved all creation – except the brown rat, which he treated with condign ferocity. He belonged to one of the recusant Catholic families, who regarded the brown rat – believed to have come over with the Hanoverians – as a symbol of their oppressed status. Consequently 'Squire' Waterton poisoned them whenever possible and on one occasion dashed out the brains of a rat, saying 'Death to all Hanoverians!' He also kept a team of ratting cats, led by a huge margay wild cat from Guyana.

In regard to all other animals he was gentleness itself, doting on hedgehogs, and having a 'special moment' in Regent's Park Zoo when the orang-utan permitted him to inspect its teeth. 'He most obligingly let me open [his mouth], and thus I had the opportunity of examining his two fine rows of teeth.'

He built a wall round Walton Hall Park, his home in Yorkshire, as a sanctuary for all the animals within it, making it the first nature reserve in England. But other aspects of his life, though equally amiable, demonstrate that he was on a trajectory that had left normality far, far behind.

It is not necessarily abnormal to climb trees. But to do so all the time, and to roost in their branches, might encourage speculation. So might sleeping in the attic with all the windows open, so that the bats and owls could come and go undisturbed. And sleeping, in addition, on the floor: 'I long learned that a bed is an absolutely useless luxury.'

He added to this a wooden pillow, but dispensed with the pillow on his travels because his suitcase served just as well. Being a guest at Walton Hall was hazardous. He often pretended to be his own butler, and would then tickle his guests with a coat brush as he helped them off with their travelling cloaks. He liked to pretend to be a dog, and bite his guests' legs as they arrived. He also cupped himself regularly 'to cure everything, from backache to malaria'. And he needed to. He paid no attention to cold or wet, and ate in a way that makes modern diets look like gluttony – a piece of toast and tea for breakfast, and a piece of bread and watercress for lunch.

He was a skilled taxidermist, and liked to 'compose' imaginary animals by combining the bits of two or more beasts. One of them, 'The Nondescript', is still on display at the Wakefield Museum, where you can also see his version of Martin Luther – a young female gorilla fitted out with horns and a disagreeable smirk. He created a tableau of reptiles dressed as famous English Protestants which does not, unhappily, survive. At the age of twenty-two he travelled to Guyana and explored the interior, reaching the Brazilian frontier trekking barefoot, alone and in the rainy season. He brought back the first specimens of curare, and having 'killed' a female donkey called Wouralia with it in an experiment, he revived her with a pair of bellows. She lived for many more years at Walton Hall.

Towards the end of his life he supplied the local lunatic asylum with telescopes so that the inmates could enjoy the wildlife in his park, and especially the waterfowl on his lake. Perhaps he felt some fellow feeling with them.

It might be mistaken to describe the fourteenth Lord Berners (1883–1950) as an animal lover, but animals certainly played a big part in his eccentricities. Better known as a composer, artist and writer, he was fictionalised as Lord Merlin in Nancy Mitford's novels. Though eccentric, he was clearly sane, and his eccentricities were thought-out and contrived – amusing, but not really barking. In childhood he heard that you could train dogs to swim by throwing them into water. He therefore threw his mother's dog out of the window to teach it to fly. It survived, but this is the only unkind act recorded of him. He was really more of a practical joker than an uncontrolled eccentric, and is perhaps a little out of place in these pages. Well, not really. For instance, he dyed the pigeons at his house at Faringdon in vibrant colours, and once gave a tea party, indoors, for Penelope Betjeman's horse. He built a 145-foot folly near his house, and secured planning permission for this only by persuading the local authority that it had no purpose at all – a category of building that did not appear on their lists. He placed a notice on it that read: 'Members of the Public committing suicide from this tower do so at their own risk'. He liked to drive round his estate in his Rolls-Royce wearing a pig's-head mask. When a young diplomat, he resented the pomposity of a senior who wound up every pronouncement by putting on his spectacles in a marked manner. Berners attached the spectacles to an ink pot, covering the senior diplomat in ink. He also pioneered the only infallible method of keeping a railway carriage to oneself. He simply sat near the door and leered horribly at every approaching passenger, at the same time beckoning them in and indicating the seat next to him. Try it. It works a treat.

Lord Bridgewater (1756–1829) gave dinner parties for dogs, dressed in the prevailing fashion and in considerable detail, even down to shoes. He did this, not occasionally, but every day. The dogs' shoes were only the start of it. He himself wore a new pair of boots or shoes every day, and had them arranged in his room in chronological order. He displayed a further oddity that will crop up again in this book – reclusiveness. For undisclosed reasons he lived in Paris for thirty years – a city that he hated. Missing England, he sometimes donned hunting pink and chased an imported fox in his Paris garden. He also kept partridges and pigeons in the garden, to shoot occasionally.

*

If the word 'reclusiveness' recurs in this book, so does the name Cavendish. The two words are combined in the person of Henry Cavendish (1731–1810). Cavendish, arguably the greatest chemist of the eighteenth century, was undoubtedly a genius. He was the first scientist to identify and manufacture hydrogen, and to combine hydrogen and oxygen to create water, and these were but two achievements in a crowded life of 'firsts'. But the peculiarities of his behaviour have led modern commentators to suggest that he may have suffered from Asperger's Syndrome. He certainly suffered from a strong aversion to other people. Confronted with an unexpected visitor, he quite simply took to his heels. He would communicate with his housekeeper only in writing, and had a separate staircase constructed so that he could avoid meeting his female servants. He shunned all social contact, although he did attend weekly scientific meetings. Other attendees were advised – if they addressed him at all – to speak into thin air within his hearing. If they were lucky they got a muttered reply.

Perhaps his greatest oddity was his shyness and carelessness about his work. One hundred years after his death, the editor of his papers was amazed to find a string of discoveries that had, in the interim, been credited to other, later comers. Among these were Richter's law of reciprocal proportions, Ohm's law, Dalton's law of partial pressures, principles of electrical conductivity (including Coulomb's law), and Charles's law of gases. Cavendish's manuscript 'Heat', dated between 1783 and 1790, was analysed in the early twenty-first century. The science historian, Russell McCormmach, has said 'Heat' is the only eighteenth-century work that prefigures thermodynamics. The theoretical physicist Dietrich Belitz has concluded that Cavendish 'got the nature of heat essentially right'.

The thing I like best about Cavendish is that he succeeded – without even leaving his house in Clapham – in weighing the earth, concluding that it tipped the scales at a hefty 13,000,000,000,000,000,000,000,000 pounds, or, in the measures of today, a little over six billion metric tonnes. Modern calculations put the earth's weight within one per cent of Cavendish's estimate.

The Cavendish Laboratory at Cambridge is named after Henry Cavendish, and was endowed by his kinsman William Cavendish, seventh Duke of Devonshire.

*

And it is to another duke that we must turn for the greatest recluse of them all – to perhaps the most eerily strange man in British history, John Cavendish Bentinck-Scott, fifth Duke of Portland (1800–1879). This gentle and sensitive man is a sympathetic figure. He did no harm, and arguably did much good in undertaking huge building projects that provided much-needed work. Early in life he was disappointed in love by the singer, Adelaide Kemble. He withdrew to his Nottinghamshire estate at Welbeck Abbey, where he lived a life that took reclusiveness to the limits of sanity.

He lived in five rooms in the Abbey, very sparsely furnished. There were 'in' and 'out' letter boxes in the door of the suite, and all his communication with the outside world was through these. Only his valet was allowed to see him in his quarters – even his doctor had to diagnose and prescribe, and even take his patient's temperature, through the door, and through the agency of the valet. His food – invariably roast chicken – was brought to him from the kitchens – a very long way away – by a little railway with heated trucks.

If he had to venture abroad all the staff and workmen on the estate had instructions not to acknowledge his presence. He was especially reluctant to meet female staff, and if one did cross his path she was immediately despatched to skate – whether she wanted to or not – on the roller-skating rink the Duke had built for the outdoor recreation of his staff. On these perambulations he wore two overcoats, a very tall top hat perched on his brown wig, and a large umbrella behind which he liked to hide. When he ventured out at night he was preceded, strangely, by a female servant 40 yards ahead of him carrying a lantern. If he had to go to London he got into his coach at the Abbey, and drove to the station where his coach was loaded bodily onto the train without his having to get out or be seen. At the other end the coach was unloaded, and the staff of his London residence had to make themselves invisible as the Duke descended from the carriage and made his way hurriedly to his study. The garden of the London house was equipped with high screens so that it could not be overlooked.

He inherited the dukedom in 1854 and put in train ambitious, extensive, and largely purposeless building schemes at Welbeck. By the time of his death there were 15,000 men employed there on his various projects. The Duke was a good employer, much liked by his men. He provided donkeys for them to ride to and from work, and umbrellas so that they could shelter from the rain. His projects included:

1. A riding school – the largest in Europe – 396 feet long, 108 feet wide, 50 feet high, and lit by 4,000 gas jets. Its walls were covered in mirrors, and the ceiling hung with crystal chandeliers. The Duke's stables held 100 horses, but not one of them ever used the riding school. Instead many antiques and paintings from the house were stored there.
2. A complex of underground tunnels. The tunnels under the estate extended to 15 miles, connecting various underground chambers and above-ground

buildings. They included a 1,000-yard-long tunnel between the house and the riding school, wide enough for several people to walk side by side. A less elaborate tunnel ran parallel to this for the use of his workmen. A 1¼ -mile-long tunnel ran from the coach house to the South Lodge, wide enough for two carriages. It had domed skylights and was additionally lit by gaslight.

3. Further underground chambers – all painted pink - included a great hall (160 by 63 feet) which was originally intended as a chapel, but which was instead designated for use as a picture gallery and occasionally as a ballroom. It could have accommodated 2,000 guests. It had a hydraulic lift that could transport 20 guests from the surface, and a ceiling that was painted as a giant sunset. No dances ever took place in the ballroom.

4. A 250-foot-long library, an observatory with a large glass roof, and a billiard room large enough to accommodate 12 billiard tables.

The only one of all these developments ever to be used was the skating rink that has already been mentioned. It is impossible to fathom what secret, ultimate plan the duke was pursuing in these projects. Nor is his treatment of the interior of his house any guide. Apart from his own Spartan apartments, he had all the rooms of Welbeck

Abbey stripped of furniture, (including antiques, tapestries and portraits; some of great value) and had it stored elsewhere, much in the riding school. By 1879 the building was in a state of disrepair, with the Duke's rooms the only habitable ones. Throughout the Abbey, all rooms were painted pink, with bare parquetry floors, and no furniture apart from a commode in one corner. That's right. Every uninhabited, pink, unfurnished room had its own loo, fully exposed to public view.

The Duke lived into his eightieth year. Few have sustained such a long life of determined oddity or projected such a powerful personal myth – whatever it was.

*

If the Duke of Portland comes first, there are many runners-up not far behind. Pursuing the Gothic undertones of Welbeck, we come to a marked vein of necrophilia among our subjects. James Lowther, first Earl of Lonsdale (1736–1802), was described by Thomas Carlyle as 'more detested than any man alive'. He was an extreme miser, treated his tenants and dependents with 'intolerable tyranny', and left a long trail of unsatisfied creditors, including the poet Wordsworth and his family. His one redeeming feature was his love for a young woman, daughter of one of his tenant farmers, whom he persuaded to elope with him. He did nothing drastic or extreme – like marry her – but he was so distressed by her death that he had her embalmed in a glass-topped coffin, which he then used as a sideboard in his dining room. He might at least have put her in the bedroom.

Where the love of a good woman stimulated Lowther's necrophiliac tendencies, with Alexander Douglas, tenth Duke of Hamilton (1767–1862) it was more the love of a good duke – in short, of himself. He thought of himself as being a very important person, and with some reason. He was not just the Duke of Hamilton He was also the Duke of Brandon, Marquess of Hamilton, Marquess of Douglas and Clydesdale, Earl of Angus, Arran, Lanark, and Selkirk, Baron Hamilton, Avon, Polmont, Mackanshire, Innerdale, Abernethy, and Jedburgh Forest, and premier peer in the peerage of Scotland; also Baron Dutton, Co. Chester, in that of Great Britain; Duke of Châtelherault in France, and hereditary keeper of Holyrood House. He thought of himself as the rightful heir to the Scottish throne. He thought a lot else of himself as well, and spent much time contemplating his own death and obsequies. In 1852 he bid against the British Museum for the sarcophagus of an Egyptian princess, and was successful, paying £11,000. It was really the only fitting resting place for a man of his importance. But not of his height. At 6-foot-6, the Duke was considerably taller than any known Egyptian princess, and he would sometimes lie disconsolately in his sarcophagus, pondering the problem. In the meantime he planned a grandiose mausoleum for all the Dukes of Hamilton at Hamilton Palace. It had a dome, inlaid marble floors, doors that were replicas of the Baptistery doors in Florence – in fact all the fixtures and fittings needed by a chap who wants to project his importance into the afterlife. He was delighted with it, and used to remark to visitors: 'What a grand sight it will be when twelve Dukes of Hamilton rise together here at the Resurrection'. (He obviously had in mind a date for the Resurrection, because we are now on the sixteenth Duke.)

The outcome of this story is sad – indeed horrid. The Duke's last words were 'Double me up! Double me up!' – referring to the lack of space in the sarcophagus. Alas, mere doubling did not meet the case, and the Duke's feet had to be removed and buried separately. Furthermore, in 1927, advances in Egyptology established that the sarcophagus was in fact intended for an Egyptian court jester – a development so apt that one is forced to wonder why God does not do this sort of thing more often. And the tenth Duke made a rod for the back of his successors, when, in the 1940s, the Inland Revenue demanded the sarcophagus in lieu of death duties. The case went to the House of Lords, and the then Duke, the fourteenth, won. (The fourteenth Duke himself deserves a mention here. He won the Scottish Middleweight amateur boxing title, led the first flight over Mount Everest in 1933, and was later embarrassed with the most unwelcome self-invited guest in history – Rudolph Hess, the Nazi Deputy Führer.) But neither he, nor any of the other dukes, will rise at the Resurrection in the tenth Duke's mausoleum, because subsidence compelled the demolition of Hamilton Palace, and the mausoleum, in 1921. Only the great sarcophagus was salvaged.

Before we plunge into the common ruck of earls and lords and whatnot, we must linger with the dukes a moment longer, because I want to absolve Andrew Robert Buxton Cavendish, eleventh Duke of Devonshire (1920–2004) from all suggestion of eccentricity. Charges of forgetfulness and shabby turnout have been laid against him. It was said of him: 'He goes out in a new suit only after his head gardener has worn it in.' So what? I have no head gardener, indeed I have no suit, but I never see a suit without thinking that what it needs most is a day's heavy digging in the rain. As for the charge of forgetfulness, the main evidence seems to be that he once forgot that he had already proposed the writer Cyril Connolly for membership of Pratts. I put it to you, members of the jury, that to forget Cyril Connolly is not true forgetfulness, but merely one of those merciful provisions of nature, like women forgetting the pain of childbirth.

Why this advocacy? Because the Duke once said in an interview with *The Spectator*: 'Most people are vain, so I try to ensure that any author who comes to stay will find at least one of their books in their room.' Such delicacy and consideration are rare indeed.

Now we must step down and mingle with the herd in the person of the thirteenth Countess of Home, mother of Alec Douglas-Home, the Prime Minister, and William Douglas-Home, the playwright. For reasons undisclosed the Countess had all her teeth removed without anaesthetic. The replacements were precarious and sometimes flew out, once into the face of an Admiral of the Fleet. When her son William was imprisoned for disobeying an order while a serving officer, she rallied round loyally and gave him the best possible advice for one facing a stretch at His Majesty's pleasure:

'Be sure to pack your evening clothes. The governor is bound to ask you to dine.'

At the completion of his sentence she wrote the governor a 'thank you' letter for having her son to stay. Later the ungrateful William attempted to alarm his mother by placing a stuffed crocodile in a stream in the grounds of The Hirsel, the family seat. Her reaction was phlegmatic in the extreme. Fixing it with a disapproving glare she remarked: 'I hadn't realised they came this far north.'

As parents, the aristocracy seem to be by turns

affectionate, negligent, and downright alarming. Most readers will be acquainted with the second Baron Redesdale (1870–1958) through the figure of Uncle Matt in the novels of his daughter, Nancy Mitford. The original is scarcely less disconcerting. It is not on record that he ever beheaded a German soldier with an entrenching tool, but surely only because there was no convenient German at hand. He hunted his daughters with bloodhounds, prospected unsuccessfully for gold on several occasions, refused to educate his daughters – other than as quarry – and was himself a stranger to the higher culture in any form. He was so upset when his wife read him *Tess of the D'Urbervilles* that she had to explain that it was fiction.

'What! The damned feller made it up?' he said, and recovered immediately.

He was enormously pleased with his far from flattering portrait in Nancy Mitford's books, especially with Uncle Matt's recurrent *leitmotif* – 'abroad is unutterably bloody and all foreigners are fiends'. He was later keenly disappointed to find that he didn't get even a walk-on part in her biography of Madame de Pompadour.

If Lord Redesdale was exposed to public view by his daughter, Victoria-Josefa, Lady Sackville (1862–1936) has been entirely eclipsed by her daughter, Vita Sackville-West. Undeservedly, because Lady Sackville displayed idiosyncrasies far more finely tuned than those of her daughter. She fluctuated between extreme parsimony and reckless extravagance. She once left a cheque for £20,000 – made out to the bearer by J. P. Morgan – in a taxi. She also liked to piece together the unmarked fragments of used stamps. Friends were often the recipients of letters written on the loo paper of Harrods's ladies room. Above all, she loved fresh air. Visitors (and there can't have been many of them) to Knole – the family's palace-sized house in Kent – had to eat outdoors, whatever the weather or season, keeping warm as best they could with rugs and hot water bottles. She never lit fires and left all windows open. If, as a result of these Spartan conditions, she should chance to catch cold, she tied a pair of socks – apparently belonging to the architect Sir Edwin Lutyens – round her neck. Her daughter Vita became a famous gardener. To vie with her, Lady Sackville used to order paper flowers by the gross and plant them out around Knole when Vita visited. She believed in dealing direct with the man at the top, and the protest she addressed to Lord Kitchener as the First World War began to eat into the manpower of Knole has to be quoted in full:

I think perhaps you do not realise, my dear Lord K, that we employ five carpenters, four painters, two blacksmiths and two footmen and you are taking them all from us! I do not complain about the footmen, although I must say I had never thought to see parlourmaids at Knole! I am sure you will sympathise with me when I say that parlourmaids are so middle-class. Not at all what you and I are used to. But I do complain about the way you take our workmen from us.

She added that under no circumstances should her husband, Lionel, be employed anywhere near the front line, since if he were killed Knole could not stand the death duties. To prepare for this frightful eventuality she used to campaign and collect for unregistered charities, of which the sole beneficiary was herself.

A different sort of wartime contretemps rose during the Second World War when the Provost of Eton, Lord Hugh Cecil, refused to countenance air-raid shelters for the boys. He had already made his opinion of shelters plain in *The Times*. Air-raid shelters, he said, 'smacked of hysteria', and added 'would it matter if a theatre full of people was bombed?' The Head Master of Eton referred the matter to the Board of Governors, and the boys of Eton got their shelters. During their tiff about this the Head Master asked the Provost, 'What would you do if a bomb did fall on the school?' Lord Hugh Cecil replied that he would ring for his butler – a man named Tucker. By great good fortune a bomb *did* fall – on the Head Master's house, and Lord Hugh *did* ring for Tucker, who presented him with his second-best hat. 'No, no.' cried his lordship. 'Me best hat to see the ruins.' He reached the Head Master's house only to find that the bomb had not exploded. His disappointment was keen. 'It's a dud!' he declared, and poked it with his stick. In the all too familiar manner of dud bombs when poked with a stick, it ceased instantly to be a dud, and exploded. There were no casualties.

All the people mentioned so far in this chapter have enjoyed a certain detachment from reality. But absolutely unfettered freedom of mind is given to few, and seems to be associated with the length of your name. William Francis Brinsley le Poer Trench, eighth Earl of Clancarty, seventh Marquess of Heusden (1911–1995) was a prominent believer in flying saucers. But not only flying saucers. He traced his own ancestry back 65,000 years to a visit by aliens, and he believed that most humans were descended from visitors from elsewhere in the universe. 'This accounts for all the different coloured skins we've got here,' he declared. However, he made an important distinction. Not all these visitors came from space. Others had emerged from tunnels dug by a still-existing civilisation below the surface of the earth. There were several such tunnels, at the Poles and at other locations like Tibet. 'I haven't been down there myself,' he said, 'but from what I gather these beings are very advanced.'

One wonders if they were advanced enough to hoist in the rest of the gospel according to Clancarty. It certainly finds me helplessly backward. In his book *The Sky People* he advances the theory that Adam and Eve, Noah and other Bible characters originated on the planet Mars. Adam and Eve were experimental creations by extraterrestrial beings. He explained that the Garden of Eden was far too nice to have been on earth, and Mars, with its delightful canals, was obviously more appropriate.

He was fortified in these convictions by meeting a US test pilot who claimed to have been at a meeting between President Eisenhower and a group of extraterrestrials at the Edwards Air Force base in 1954. Their spacecraft were saucer shaped with the exception of two that were cigar shaped. The aliens looked a bit like humans but not exactly.

Beside this Sir Hugh Rankin (1899–1988) was the palest of neophytes. The best he could come up with was: 'It is part of our known belief that five Bodhisattvas [Perfected Men] control the destiny of the world. They meet once a year in a cave in the Himalayas to make their decisions. One of them lives in the Scottish Cairngorms.'

We come finally to Sir George Reresby Sitwell (1860–1943). Even the normally discreet and buttoned-up *Concise Dictionary of National Biography* breaks out with: 'erratic and difficult parent of Osbert, Sacheverell and Edith Sitwell'. That is to put it mildly. Small wonder that all the three children displayed marked eccentricities themselves, and that each left a memoir of their peculiar parent.

It is not only that he invented a pistol for shooting wasps. Like the tenth Duke of Hamilton he was inordinately proud of his social position. This surfaced at the age of four, in a railway carriage, when he informed the company that 'I am Sir George Reresby Sitwell, the youngest baronet in England'. Later in life, taking a guest for a stroll on the terrace at Renishaw (the Sitwell home), he gestured expansively at the landscape and said, with the deepest satisfaction, 'Nothing between us and the Lockyer-Lambtons'. Renishaw is in Derbyshire, and there were, of course, many villages, mines, and even a small town between Renishaw and the Lockyer-Lambtons – but not in Sir George's eyes.

With less family pride, and a larger helping of intellect, Sir George might have been something like a Renaissance Man. He wrote continuously and compulsively. His writings, almost entirely unpublished, filled seven rooms at Renishaw. Here is a sampling of their titles: *Wool-Gathering in Medieval Times and Since*, *Lepers' Squints*, *Domestic Manners in Sheffield in the Year 1250*, *Acorns as an Article of Medieval Diet*, *The History of the Fork*, *The History of the Cold* and *The*

Errors of Modern Parents. His one published work was about landscape gardening – the sole area in which he can be seen as an expert. *On the Making of Gardens* appeared in 1909.

Unable to find a publisher for any of his other writings, Sir George bought a press and printed many of them himself. He never attempted fiction, which he believed to be deleterious to the health. He advised his son Osbert not to write a novel, saying: 'You'd better drop that idea at once. My cousin Stephen Arlington had a friend who utterly ruined his health writing a novel.' As far as his own health was concerned, he was a hypochondriac, travelling with a vast array of medicines, all inaccurately labelled to prevent anyone else using them.

He possessed great estates, and took a keen interest in them, not necessarily agricultural. Cows, it struck him, were not decorative creatures, and he attempted to improve their appearance by stencilling them with the Chinese Willow Pattern. His son Sacheverell was almost expelled from Eton when his father demanded to pay his fees in farm produce. Later in life Sir George's landscape-gardening ambitions broke out uncontrollably while visiting his younger son, Sacheverell. 'I don't propose to do much here. Just a sheet of water and a line of statues.'

Along with the Wasp Pistol, he invented a musical toothbrush, sent peach stones to the War Office in the belief that they could be used in gas masks, corrected Albert Einstein on several errors he detected in the General Theory of Relativity, and had a valet called Moat who owned a pet seal. He is famous for the sign he put up at Renishaw, visible to all guests: 'I must ask anyone entering the house never to contradict me in any way, as it interferes with the functioning of the gastric juices and prevents my sleeping at night.'

(At least one of his children, Osbert, attempted a small act of revenge. He doctored the prospectus of a private mental institution to make it look like a luxury hotel. Sir George enthusiastically agreed to spend a fortnight there. The booking was made. Unfortunately the proprietor wrote back, 'Ought a strait-waistcoat to be sent for Sir George to wear during the journey, which will be made by van? Three strong and practised nurses will, of course, be in attendance, and prepared to quell any disturbance by the way.')

Sir George married, in 1886, Ida Emily Augusta Denison. He refused to pay off her many creditors, preferring to see her prosecuted, and imprisoned for three months.

He gets no more than a passing mention in his daughter's famous book, *English Eccentrics* – not perhaps the least of the family's abounding eccentricities.

'Westminster . . . had no difficulty in producing highly incriminating evidence against Beauchamp. In spite of its detailed and specific nature, Lady Beauchamp remained mystified. "Bendor says that Beauchamp is a bugler," she complained in bewilderment.'

SEX AT THE TOP

Hunnish scenes, sheikhs and buglers

Second only to the field sports (of which it often seems to be one) sex is the subject that has most preoccupied the upper classes. Indeed the sheer quantity of material could easily overwhelm a slim volume like this, so I have confined myself to what seem to me to be the interesting and unusual aspects of posh couplings. The first thing to say is that there was an awful lot of it about. In the words of Queen Victoria: 'I fear the seventh granddaughter and fourteenth grandchild becomes a very uninteresting thing – for it seems to go on like the rabbits in Windsor Park.'

And you can't have children without coupling. For most of history it has also been very difficult to couple without having children, and the fact that the rich had enough money to cushion themselves against the consequences of pregnancy is one of the reasons that in times that were periods of sexual restraint for other people, the aristocracy managed to keep at it – as Queen Victoria said – like rabbits.

And not only procreational sex, because both genders of homosexuality are well represented – and bi-sexuality. But there is another aspect of sex that concerns the upper classes more than other people – the need for legitimate heirs, or heirs that can be passed off as legitimate. Hence the obligation to produce 'an heir and a spare' before a lady could please herself in her choice of lovers.

All the yeasty currents of upper-class sex met in the 1920s in what became known as the Ampthill Baby case – in which not only the issues of legitimacy and inheritance were thrashed out, but even the possibility of virgin birth as a consequence of *fertilisatio ab abstracto*.

John Russell was the heir to the Ampthill Barony. Known as 'Stilts' because of his height – 6 foot 6 inches – he was a junior naval officer when, in 1917, he proposed to Christabel Hart whom he had met by placing an advertisement in *The Times*. She accepted him, but then changed her mind, saying she 'was not the marrying kind'. Her real interests were hunting and partying. She excelled at the tango. She abruptly eloped to Scotland with Russell's best friend, but the Scots authorities were too canny to let them get married, and she returned the next day, writing to Russell to say that she would marry him after all. 'I thought it would be nice and peaceful not to be pestered by men asking me to marry them,' she later explained.

They were married on 18 October 1918, in Kensington, West London, but only on Christabel's terms. Christabel insisted on separate bedrooms and delivered an ultimatum on the eve of the wedding: she did not want children, and her husband should abstain from 'anything that could cause pregnancy'. He agreed, but he made attempts, rather pathetic ones, to change her mind. For instance when his submarine docked at Greenock, he sent her Marie Stopes's book *Married Love*, containing contraceptive advice. She did not like the use of 'preventives of conception', she angrily replied. She bombarded him with cheery letters about her successes with men. 'I need hardly say your wife has a vast following of adoring young men. I've four in the Bucks Light Infantry.' She claimed to be 'in love with a Dago young man' who had 'lovely hands' and boasted of dancing with 'dark sleek Argentinians... Your very naughty wife'. In two years the couple dined together only twice.

Russell underwent the full tally of humiliations that a self-centred and lively young woman can inflict on a doting man. The only time he was allowed into her bedroom was to bring her breakfast in bed, when she would regale him with the details of her previous night out. On one occasion a friend rang him in the morning and asked him to bring round day clothes for Christabel, who had spent the night there.

Russell's parents detested Christabel, but invited the couple to the Ampthill estate in Bedfordshire in December 1920. They put them in the same room. That night, the unhappy Russell did try to consummate his marriage, in circumstances that were later described by Christabel as 'Hunnish scenes'. She said of that night 'he attempted to effect penetration but I would not allow it'.

Within a month she went to stay with her racehorse trainer, Captain Lionel Cross, stopping at the same hotel in Salisbury in adjoining rooms. Russell had had enough. In early 1921, on his mother's advice, he decided to annul the marriage on the grounds of non-consummation. Christabel stopped wearing her wedding ring and they lived apart, at any rate for a bit. But in June 1921, she suddenly changed her mind. She met her husband in London, and bizarrely informed him that he was prone to fits of sleepwalking. She then announced that she was pregnant – presumably as a result of one of these 'sleepwalking' episodes. The ever-credulous Russell was delighted:

'I am most awfully happy about the baby,' he wrote to

her. 'If only you had told me (about the sleepwalking) I would have padlocked myself to my bed… I am very sorry.'

Up to this point it is easy to regard Christabel as simply a good-time girl, with an idiot of a husband, and an inventive line in excuses. But now the astonishing fact emerged – the same doctor who found her to be pregnant, also declared her to be *virgo intacta.* At least a bit *intacta.* 'An only partly perforated hymen' was the precise description. 'I suppose I must be another Virgin Mary,' wrote Christabel to Russell.

Under intense pressure from his parents, Russell at last came to his senses. 'Nothing short of a miracle would make it possible for us both to have been unaware that we had conjugal relations,' he replied. He sued for divorce, citing three men.

The case began in July 1922, nine months after the birth of Christabel's child, Geoffrey, on 15 October 1921. (The child's birth was itself nine months after she had stayed in a hotel with Captain Cross, and ten months after the 'Hunnish scenes' with her husband.) During the hearing Christabel was asked to write down all the occasions on which she had 'slept over' at other men's addresses. She admitted to four. But she insisted that on no occasion did anything improper happen. She testified that she had no idea what the male member was for, nor that it could change size. She simply preferred the company of other men to that of her husband who disgusted her by dressing in women's clothes. The court was shown pictures. Russell explained that these were taken at fancy dress parties, but he admitted that he did sometimes cross-dress for fun, and that he had a female wardrobe at home, complete with stockings and stays.

Medical men testified (a) that Christabel had never had full intercourse with a man, (b) that conception was possible without penetration (*fertilisatio ab abstracto*), and (c) that a ten-month term was possible. They also raised the tantalising possibility that Christabel might have inadvertently impregnated herself by 'injudiciously' using the same bath sponge as her husband. What had he been up to? Russell's nanny and his shipmates testified that he never sleepwalked.

So, what on earth really happened? I think we can discount the sponge. 'Hunnish scenes' might well include ejaculation between a woman's thighs, close enough to the opening of the vagina to allow one of those active, wriggly little chaps to make a home run – but that could have occurred as easily with one of her 'sleep overs' as with her husband. It was all very baffling, and no surprise that, after a ten-day hearing, the jury failed to reach a verdict.

A retrial found Christabel guilty and declared her child illegitimate. She appealed, lost, and appealed again to the House of Lords to establish her son's legitimacy as heir to the Ampthill title. On each occasion the details of the case were thrashed out again, moving the King, George V, to declare the whole thing 'worse than the pages of the most extravagant French novel'. It was probably the first time their Lordships had been asked to ponder the matter of virgin birth. They found for Christabel on the grounds that 'no child born after a marriage could be declared illegitimate merely on the testimony of his mother or father'. O what a tangled web we weave, when first we practise to conceive.

Russell divorced Christabel, and inherited the Ampthill title in 1935. He remarried and had a son, John. Christabel retired to Ireland and devoted herself to fox hunting, becoming joint Master of the Ballymacad Hunt in County Meath. Russell died in 1973, and John claimed the title. Geoffrey Russell, Christabel's child, contested the claim, and won, but not before obliging their Lordships to go through the whole process of splitting heirs again.

From the distance of the twenty-first century it is impossible to review the Ampthill Baby case without some levity. But it is equally impossible not to feel sympathy and even sadness for the two protagonists. They simply had no idea what they were up to – launched into an era of increasing sexual freedom with no sexual knowledge or education at all. At the time of the trial

Christabel did admit to a friend, 'I have been indiscreet all my life and he [Russell] has enough evidence to divorce me once a week.' But what did she mean by this? It doesn't stack up with the evidence of her virginity.

Her grandson, Anthony Russell, has written feelingly about his upbringing and his grandmother. His judgement seems to me to be the most realistic and likely – that she had not committed adultery and had an aversion to sex. 'She infinitely preferred brushing down one of her hunters... to even contemplating the act of physical intimacy with a man,' he says.

Am I succumbing helplessly to rural myth in speculating that the hunters of her childhood may have been responsible for her 'partly perforated hymen'?

*

To find a lady wholly at ease with her sexuality we can turn to Jane Digby (1807–81). Unlike Christabel Hart she did not in the least mind being pestered by men, and enjoyed a career of considerable sexual adventurousness. She was accounted a great beauty, 'tall, with a perfect figure. She had a lovely face, pale-gold hair, wide-spaced dark blue eyes, long dark lashes, and a wild rose complexion.' To the modern taste her portrait looks more pert and sexy than beautiful, with an extremely 'come hither' look in her eye.

She married first Lord Ellenborough, in 1819, but

soon embarked on affairs with her cousin, Colonel George Anson (whom she thought to be the father of her son), and Prince Felix Schwarzenberg, an attaché at the Austrian embassy in London. She bore Schwarzenberg two children, and Ellenborough divorced her, amid much scandal, by Act of Parliament in 1830. Schwarzenberg promptly deserted her, earning him the London nickname of Prince of Cadland.

She then began what was to become a lifetime's occupation – man-hopping, but always in an easterly direction, scattering children as she went. She moved to Munich and, with a sure instinct for seeking out the top, became the mistress of King Ludwig I of Bavaria. But in 1832 she made a marriage of convenience to Baron Karl von Venningen, another Bavarian. It must have been very convenient, because she bore him two children before, in 1838, taking a Greek, Count Spyridon Theotokis, as her next lover. Venningen challenged Theotokis to a duel, and wounded him. Honour satisfied, Venningen released Jane from her marriage, and they remained on good terms for the rest of their lives. Jane joined the Greek Orthodox Church, married Theotokis, moved to Greece, and bore him a son. This unhappy lad died in a fall from a balcony and the couple divorced in 1846, leaving Jane free to move up once more and engulf the Greek King, Otto – the son of her previous lover, King Ludwig – as her next amour. Perhaps because she found yet another Bavarian a bit heavy going, she next attached her affections to a hero of the Greek revolution, General Christodoulos Chatzpetros. She campaigned with him, living in caves, riding horses and acting as the self-appointed 'queen' of his brigand army. She left him when she discovered that he had been unfaithful to her, which is a bit rich.

Finally, in 1853, at the age of forty-six, she travelled to Syria, and fell in love with Sheikh Mijwal al-Musrab, twenty-five years her junior. She took like a duck to water to tribal life, adopting Arab dress, adding Arabic to the other eight languages she spoke, and participating in tribal raids and other skirmishes. She built a palace in Damascus, where, between intervals of nomadic tribal life, she spent the rest of her life, meeting and befriending Richard and Isabel Burton when he was the British Consul there. Other European visitors to Damascus attested that her appearance and beauty remained unchanged with the years, but then they had been travelling through the desert for some weeks. Her marriage to the Sheikh was happy, and lasted the rest of her life. It also remained active. Like many Victorian ladies, Jane kept a diary. The entry for her seventieth birthday read: 'It is now some three days since the Sheikh graced my bed. What can be the matter?'

*

At the time, Jane Digby's career was highly scandalous, but at least it could be talked about – albeit in hushed tones. During the nineteenth century and most of the twentieth, century homosexuality, especially female homosexuality, could hardly be mentioned at all. Female homosexuality never became illegal – allegedly because none of her ministers had the nerve to present a bill mentioning these practices to Queen Victoria – and female couples found it easier to set up house and live together than their male counterparts. But in a strange way male homosexuality, though illegal, dangerous, and the target of much virulent prejudice, managed to secure a higher public profile, and to be, at any rate among the more relaxed sections of society, more openly referred to. In spite of this, right up to the 1960s and beyond, public exposure as a homosexual could wreck a man's career and destroy his private life.

Such was the fate of William Lygon, seventh Earl Beauchamp, KG, KCMG, PC (1872–1938). The model for Lord Marchmain in Evelyn Waugh's *Brideshead Revisited*, Beauchamp enjoyed a career of public success from an early age. At only twenty-seven he was appointed Governor of New South Wales, provoking Belloc's lines 'But as it is, my language fails/*Go out and govern New South Wales!*' Other posts followed. In 1902, Beauchamp joined the Liberal Party and in the same year he married Lady Lettice Mary Elizabeth Grosvenor, daughter of

Victor Grosvenor, Earl Grosvenor, son of the first Duke of Westminster. In 1905, when the Liberals came to power, he was appointed Captain of the Honourable Corps of Gentlemen-at-Arms, and sworn onto the Privy Council. He further became Lord Steward of the Household, Lord President of the Council, and First Commissioner of Works. He was also Lord Lieutenant of Gloucestershire, Lord Warden of the Cinque Ports and a Knight of the Garter.

This accomplished courtier and public servant was a family man, devoted to his seven children. But he was also a flamboyantly indiscreet homosexual, with a particular taste for footmen and a vibrant sex life of almost rococo elaboration. During his term as Governor, the New South Wales press did not fail to note that all the servants at Government House were young, male, and exceedingly decorative. The Governor 'has exquisite taste in footmen,' commented one journalist. When interviewing young men for jobs he would run his hands over their buttocks, making noises 'similar to a groom rubbing down a horse'. The footmen at his English house, Madresfield, wore so many diamond rings and other jewellery that guests could hear them clinking as they served dinner. The writer Harold Nicolson recalls a dinner at Madresfield when Lord Beauchamp murmured to his butler, *'Je t'adore!'* A scandalised guest overheard, and was appeased only when Nicolson said – with a promptness that did credit to his wits – 'I think he said "shut the door".' And Nicolson – no slouch himself in this respect – also attested that the butler was indeed an exceptionally good-looking man.

As they grew older, Beauchamp's children learnt to warn any male friends to lock their bedroom doors when they came to stay, and there were occasions when Lord Beauchamp was caught *in flagrante* – once when a servant, looking through a keyhole, observed him and his doctor 'engaged' on the sofa; and again when he was seen giving fellatio to – you've guessed – a footman. When Warden of the Cinque Ports, he held parties for Kentish lads, fishermen and prominent homosexuals from London at Walmer Castle. A visitor to his London house was staggered to meet the actor, Ernest Thesiger, naked from the waist up and swathed in ropes of pearls. The same guest – who seems to have been a bit slow on the uptake – visited Madresfield and was puzzled to find that the very beautiful 'tennis coach' barely knew how to hold a racquet. And on a subsequent tour of Australia, in 1930, Beauchamp took a 'secretary' and a young valet who were both patently co-habiting with him. The novelist Hugh Walpole reported seeing him at 'the baths at the Elephant and Castle in the act with a boy'.

Tastes so publicly indulged could scarcely be kept a secret, and indeed Beauchamp's inclinations were a matter of common knowledge in his own circle. But

Beauchamp was able to live his double life undisturbed, until he was overtaken by nemesis in the person of his brother-in-law, the second Duke of Westminster, known to his friends as Bendor.

Westminster was an unattractive mix of womaniser and prude. When rumours about Beauchamp's life became too persistent, he took up the cudgels on behalf of his sister Lettice, the Countess Beauchamp. You may wonder what part she had played up to this point. The fact is that she was so unworldly – some would say so stupid – that she simply didn't understand what her husband was doing. One of her children said that even at the end of her life she hadn't really grasped the nature of his predilections.

Westminster set out to destroy Beauchamp, and, so he hoped, being himself a Tory, the Liberal Party as well. He already had reason to dislike Beauchamp. Banned from Court on the grounds of his divorce, Westminster resented Beauchamp's public success. Beauchamp had produced male heirs. He had not, in spite of three marriages. (His only son died of appendicitis and peritonitis.) Above all he resented the fact that Beauchamp's entirely illegal love life seemed to have no adverse effect on his marriage or career.

During Beauchamp's 1930 Australian tour his relationship with his secretary and valet became known in London. Westminster reported this to King George V, who replied 'I thought men like that shot themselves.' (I hope readers will agree with me that when George V is around one is never short of a good quote. Another version gives the King's reply as 'I thought men only did that sort of thing abroad.') Westminster employed private detectives, who had no difficulty in producing highly incriminating evidence against Beauchamp. In spite of its detailed and specific nature, Lady Beauchamp remained mystified. 'Bendor says that Beauchamp is a bugler,' she complained in bewilderment.

Bendor himself left no doubt. 'Dear Bugger in Law,' he wrote to Beauchamp. 'You have got what you deserved.'

Lady Beauchamp took her brother's advice, left Beauchamp, and in due course divorced him. Her children remained loyal to their father, and never forgave their mother. But Bendor was baulked of full victory. Beauchamp's close connection to Court made the King strongly averse to any open scandal. Furthermore, Beauchamp's own daughter, Sibell, by this time a worldly young woman and mistress of the Canadian press baron, Lord Beaverbrook, persuaded her lover to 'kill the story', which he successfully did, both in his own papers and in all the others.

The Beauchamp divorce received little publicity, and Beauchamp himself was allowed to resign his posts and retire abroad. Bendor's evidence, however, remained 'live', and the threat of prosecution hung over Beauchamp if he should ever return. In 1936 his second son died and Beauchamp was determined to attend the funeral at Madresfield, regardless of the risk of arrest. Once again the redoubtable Sibell leant on her lover and persuaded him to use his influence to suspend the warrant against Beauchamp. The warrant was suspended, indeed later annulled, but Beauchamp continued to live abroad until his death of cancer in New York in 1938.

Astonishingly, Sibell went on to contract, first a bigamous, and later a legal marriage, to Michael Rowley, Bendor's stepson. In the circumstances one doesn't know quite what to make of Lord Beaverbrook's comment: 'Buy Old Masters. They fetch a better price than old mistresses.'

*

Female homosexuality, if not exactly tolerated, was legal and less visible. Mention of it remained taboo for a long time, and Radclyffe Hall's novel *The Well of Loneliness* (1928) was prosecuted for obscenity and banned. However, so long as they kept their heads below the parapet, lesbian women could live together without fear of legal reprisals and without much fear of adverse comment. It would be quite wrong to classify anyone's sexual inclinations as eccentric *per se*, but at least one thorough eccentric was also a lesbian – or so most authorities agree.

SEX AT THE TOP

Marie Corelli (1855–1924) was a British novelist, and a stunningly successful one – at least in terms of sales. Her novels sold more copies than the sales of all her popular contemporaries combined – and this included some spectacular sales heavyweights like Arthur Conan Doyle, H. G. Wells, and Rudyard Kipling. She was Queen Victoria's favourite author and her works were collected by King Edward VII, the future King George V and by Winston and Randolph Churchill, amongst others. Other than William Shakespeare she is the only writer to have a plaque in Stratford-on-Avon, where she lived for many years. She is now almost completely forgotten, which is a pity, because, good writer or bad, she was engagingly absurd.

Born Mary Mackay, the illegitimate daughter of a Scottish poet called Dr Charles Mackay by his housemaid Elizabeth Mills, Corelli was educated in France, which prompted her choice of pseudonym. Her novels reflect an attempt to reconcile orthodox Christian belief with a number of even more batty preoccupations – like reincarnation and astral projection, very fashionable at the time. She has sometimes been hailed as the progenitor of New Age religion. In spite, or because, of their huge popularity, her books got a pasting from the critics, best summed up in James Agate's judgement: 'the imagination of a Poe with the style of an Ouida and the mentality of a nursemaid'. The critic Grant Allen wrote: 'a woman of deplorable talent who imagined that she was a genius, and was accepted as a genius by a public to whose commonplace sentimentalities and prejudices she gave a glamorous setting.'

Corelli was almost certainly the original for 'Lucia' in E. F. Benson's novels. The small-town snobbery; the pretence of being a great artist and musician; the pretence of speaking fluent Italian – all these were recorded of Corelli. But even E. F. Benson did not go as far as his original when she imported a gondola, plus attendant gondolier, to row her up and down the Avon at Stratford.

For forty years of her life Corelli lived with Bertha Vyer. Some have denied that they were lovers, but their initials were carved intertwined over the fireplace at her Stratford house, representing the symbol of life, and her novels are full of descriptions of female beauty that verge on the unashamedly erotic. Whatever her orientation, she once committed to paper an opinion of marriage, which should delight all feminists – and indeed all women: 'I never married because there was no need. I have three pets at home which answer the same purpose as a husband. I have a dog which growls every morning, a parrot which swears all afternoon and a cat that comes home late at night.'

It is fitting that E. F. Benson should have memorialised her, albeit fictionally. His own mother, Mary Benson, was the better half of one of the most peculiar partnerships in Victorian England. While her husband, Edward Benson, fought the good fight against his own, male, homosexual tendencies, Mary was able to let rip her female homosexuality. This included a lesbian love triangle in which she competed with her own daughter, Nellie, for the love of a shared girlfriend, and a later liaison which drove another of Mary's offspring to try to murder her. There were also many, many other attachments as Mary's feelings for other women, which she called 'swarmings', got the better of her. Some went unrequited, while others reached what she described as 'a complete fusing'.

She was discreet about these affairs, and she had need to be. Because Edward, after a progression of other appointments, became Archbishop of Canterbury, and much of Mary's love life was conducted within the sacred precincts of Lambeth Palace. But she was surely entitled to her indulgences, because she was the victim – I do not think that is too strong a term – of her husband's extraordinary, some might say creepy, behaviour. Recognising his own latent homosexuality while still a young man, he hit on the ploy of 'courting' Mary – then only eleven – as an antidote, possibly a cure. In a process that would now be called grooming, he set out to make Mary his ideal partner. With her mother's consent (astonishingly) the couple were engaged while she was still twelve, although they did not marry until she was eighteen. Her diary records her dismay on her wedding night: 'How my heart sank, knowing that I felt nothing of what I knew people ought to feel. Trying to be rapturous, not succeeding, feeling so inexpressibly lonely and young.'

It also records her affairs, listing them by number. Of number 39 she wrote:

'O that sweet time with Emily. How we drew together. Lord, it was Thou, teaching me how to love.'

It is always helpful to have God on your side.

She died in bed with her maid of the moment, Lucy Tait.

*

Before we leave the shores of homosexuality in favour of the hurly-burly of heterosexual carryings-on, it is useful to remember that, however taboo the subject, most people (Lettice Beauchamp excepted) knew what was going on and often said so.

Embarking on a channel crossing, Osbert Sitwell and Harold Nicolson (the bisexual husband of Vita Sackville-West, *see* pp. 93, 94, 199) were asked to fill in embarkation forms.

'What age are you going to put, Osbert?' asked Nicolson.

'What sex are you going to put, Harold?' was the reply.

And Lady Tree, wife of the actor Sir Herbert Beerbohm Tree, and herself an actress, was certainly aware both of her husband's weaknesses, and those of others. Dining with her one evening the author, Somerset Maugham, left early, excusing himself with the words, 'I must look after my youth.' Lady Tree replied, 'Next time do bring him. We adore those sort of people.' On another occasion she surprised her husband dining alone with a young actor, Esme Percy, a man of considerable good looks. 'Enjoy your supper, Mr Percy,' she said. 'The port is on the chimney piece, and don't forget – it's still adultery.'

And finally from Archibald, fifth Earl of Rosebery, rather a risqué example for a married man, a prime minister, whose family name was 'Primrose', and who had already been hounded (like Oscar Wilde) by the ninth Marquess of Queensberry for an alleged association with Queensberry's son, who was Rosebery's private secretary: 'All my life I've loved a womanly woman and admired a manly man, but I never could stand a boily boy.'

*

Back to the straights. Apart from encounters in brothels and houses of assignation, the main stamping ground for upper-class sex was the country house – particularly the country house parties that became such a marked feature of late Victorian and Edwardian life. It was a wise hostess who knew who was 'with' whom and arranged the bedrooms accordingly. Many a long trek was undertaken in the small hours to reach the right room, not always fruitfully, as Lord Rossmore (1892–1958) recalled:

Once I was invited to a country house where a lovely lady whom I greatly admired was also a guest. We were delighted to meet in this accidentally-done-for-the-purpose manner and arranged to have a tête-à-tête later to look at the stars. Well, I must have dropped off to sleep, because I was horrified to find it was 3 a.m., when I set out down the ghostly corridor to keep my appointment. I padded along and turned down the passage which led to the room where we planned to meet, but when I got there I noticed a man sitting on guard outside. He viewed me with a lowering brow, and then I grasped the fact that as he had not been asked to stargaze he was determined to see who had. I pretended not to notice him, and walked on to the bathroom, where I took an early tub, and thought of many things I should like to have said to him.

Similarly frustrated, but more dramatically, was Lord Charles Beresford. Hoping to surprise his mistress, he burst into her room, jumped onto the bed, beating his chest and crowing 'cock-a-doodle-doo!' The occupants of the bed, the Bishop of Chester and his wife, were unamused. He had simply lost the way.

It was not only illicit sex that posed problems in the country house. Daisy, Princess of Pless, recalls sleeping in separate rooms from her husband at her family home, Newlands: 'There was something unusual in his having to come right along a passage, past other doors, and then leave quietly on tiptoe as if he (and I too) had been doing something wrong; there is a little air of mystery about it which is amusing, and therefore more tempting.' The temptation must have been very great, because when Daisy first married Hans Heinrich, Prince of Pless, and went to live at Fürstenstein, his castle in East Prussia, it was she who had to make the journey – a very long one – from her room to his, through the ancient and rambling castle, preceded and followed by footmen bearing candelabra. It must certainly have added a sense of occasion.

There was a less light-hearted side to country-house sex. With so many young female domestic servants, it was inevitable that the men in the house would sometimes be attracted by them. There may have been some fruitful and loving master/servant relationships, but for the most part the girl was – often heavily – the loser. In the unjust manner of the times, it was she who took the blame if discovered.

Ethel ('Ettie'), Lady Desborough (1867–1952), a noted

beauty, prominent member of The Souls, and described as 'the last great Whig hostess', gave many and frequent house parties at Taplow Court, on the Thames near Marlow. On one such occasion she was woken early by her housekeeper who told her that one of the maids – Effie – had been found in the bed of one of the male guests. Pausing only to check that the guest had been in the bed at the same time, Ettie summoned Effie and fired her. The girl's mother was warned to collect her from the train, and Lady Desborough undertook not to 'tell' if she was approached by a prospective employer. She also gave Effie £5 – about £366 in today's money.

Later Lady Desborough was having her morning tea in the conservatory, when the male guest approached her – neatly dressed in a linen suit, sporting a gardenia in his button hole, and twirling his moustache. He greeted his hostess with a kiss and said: 'Mornin', Lady D. I hear you fired the little culprit.'

Almost the most disturbing aspect of this story is that Lady Desborough, by the standards of the time, behaved generously and kindly to the girl. The guest was not asked to leave.

He has been identified as Harry Cust (Henry Cockayne-Cust, 1861–1917; *see also* p. 63), a man so uncontrollably philoprogenitive that he is thought to have fathered a large proportion of the British aristocracy of that generation, among them Lady Diana Cooper and

Clementine Hozier (Winston Churchill's wife). In her book *The Marlborough House Set*, Anita Leslie writes: 'So much of the Cust strain entered England's peerage . . . that from . . . a number of cradles there gazed babies with eyes like large sapphires instead of the black boot buttons of their legal fathers.'

So far as women were concerned, Cust was undeniably a rotter. In the summer of 1893 he seduced his future wife, Nina Welby-Gregory, who became pregnant. He was engaged to another woman at the time, and was staying at her house when he got a letter from Nina, desperate at her plight, and imploring his help. He read this letter out loud in the smoking room of his fiancée's house, commenting on it heartlessly and facetiously. His listeners were disgusted, and his family compelled him to marry Nina. In spite of a lifetime of behaviour like this, Cust remained irresistibly attractive to women, demonstrating that, whatever gentlemen may prefer, blondes like cads. No doubt it is all part of their subconscious attempts to marry their fathers.

Cust's bright, piercing blue eyes lend weight to even further speculation as to his powers of paternity. Margaret Thatcher's grandmother, Mrs Phoebe Stephenson, was a housemaid at Belton near Grantham, Cust's family home. Her daughter, Mrs Thatcher's mother, was born on 24 August 1888, which would date her conception in about December 1887, when Cust was twenty-six. Lady

Diana Cooper, a child of Cust 'on the wrong side of the sheets' (see above), jokingly referred to Lady Thatcher as 'my niece'. An additional irony is that Thatcher happily borrowed silver and other appointments from Belton to embellish 10 Downing Street.

Servants tended to assume the morality of their employers. I have it on the authority of the late Geoffrey Castle that when, short of cash, he took service as a gentleman's private gentleman (aka a valet), matters below stairs were regulated like matters above stairs – only better. When he and his employer arrived at a country house, the butler took him under his wing and assigned one of the female staff as his companion for the weekend. How they interpreted 'companionship' was up to them.

Sir Ralph Payne-Gallwey (1848–1916) was certainly an habitué of country houses. Indeed he owned one, Thirkleby Hall, in Yorkshire. More properly he belongs to the sporting chapter of this book, being a lifelong shootist, and the author of books with titles like *High Pheasants in Theory and Practice*, *Letters to Young Shooters*, *A Little Plain Law for Game Preservers, Keepers and Poachers* and *Swivel Guns, Breechloaders and Muzzleloaders*. More or less a ballistics maniac, how does he earn his place in a chapter on sex? Solely to demonstrate that the Victorians were not always as buttoned-up as we suppose. Returning by train from

London to his Yorkshire home, he shared a carriage with an aloof and taciturn lady of a certain age. Even so noted a charmer as Sir Ralph could not get a word out of her, and both parties eventually fell asleep. As he got out at York, he turned to the lady and said: 'We might not have had much conversation, but at least we can say we have slept together.'

In the same vein is the comment of Lord Castlerosse (1891–1943). A gossip columnist, bon viveur and womaniser, Castlerosse was also vastly fat. A woman, meeting him for the first time, was so startled by his size that she said: 'Lord Castlerosse, if that stomach was on a woman I would say she was pregnant.'

'Madam,' came the magnificent reply, 'half an hour ago it was, and she is!'

And perhaps the best way to conclude this chapter is with a series of quotations throwing light on the greater-than-supposed freedom of our forebears.

Tallulah Bankhead (1902–68), the smouldering Southern belle and Hollywood star, may not seem at first sight have much to do with the eccentricities of the British upper crust. She famously revealed to *Motion Picture Magazine* in 1932:

> I'm serious about love. I'm damned serious about it now . . . I haven't had an affair for six months. Six months! Too long . . . If there's anything the matter with me now, it's not Hollywood or Hollywood's

state of mind . . . The matter with me is, I WANT A MAN! . . . Six months is a long, long while. I WANT A MAN!

Unleashed in England during her stint on the London stage in the early twenties, this spirit had disturbing consequences. Even the security service, MI5, was involved, being called in to investigate reports that Bankhead had seduced up to half a dozen pupils at the famous public school, Eton College, persuading them to take part in 'indecent and unnatural' acts. The report was hushed up. Among her other conquests in England was 'Bendor' Westminster (*see* pp. 12, 59, 69, 116–17). Many years later he encountered her again in the famous '43' club, and greeted her warmly, perhaps too warmly.

'I thought I told you to wait in the car,' was her reaction.

If Bankhead had a single, serious love, it was the bi-sexual British peer, Lord Alington, whom she adored. At some time during their on-off relationship, he cut her when he was dining in the same restaurant with another woman. Bankhead was having none of that. She approached, and said sweetly: 'Don't you recognise me with my clothes on?'

One more from this irresistible woman, to another, unnamed English lover: 'I'll come and make love to you at five o'clock. If I'm late, start without me.'

In 1973 Lord Lambton (1922–2006) found himself

embroiled in a scandal after a call girl, Norma Levy, had recorded his conversations with her using a microphone hidden in the nose of her teddy bear, while her husband filmed the encounter through a two-way mirror. The ensuing rumpus nearly toppled the Edward Heath government. Reflecting in some bewilderment on the affair, Lambton said: 'I can't think what all the fuss is about; surely all men visit whores?'

The goings-on of the Happy Valley set in Kenya in the twenties and thirties were unquestionably upper class, and very highly coloured. Lady Idina Sackville, stepping out of her onyx bath to greet guests stark naked, must have been quite a spectacle, although her photographs and portrait show, to the modern taste, an unattractive woman. But because of the obtrusion of drugs, their conduct seems more sordid than eccentric. They gave rise to the suitably feeble quip: 'Are you married, or do you live in Kenya?'

But the mention of East Africa brings us to the last word on upper-class sex. When Lord Snowdon's marriage to Princess Margaret fell apart, he was reassured by a well-wisher: 'Your experience will be a lesson to all us men to be careful not to marry ladies in very high positions.'

These pearls of wisdom dropped from the lips of Idi Amin, President of Uganda, and blood-soaked tyrant.

'He was, indeed, the last British soldier to kill an enemy with a
longbow – a German NCO in 1940 in a French village.'

MILITARY MADNESS

'Stop dying at once, and when you get up,
get a bloody hair cut!'

Warfare – like hunting but on a vaster scale – is lunacy unleashed, and the profession of arms has a tendency to attract men whose grasp on normal reality is not very firm. It was also the waste bin to which the aristocracy consigned their less-gifted younger sons, giving the British army a sort of amateur colouring at the edges – a margin where thoroughly wayward behaviour could flourish. But in a contradictory way the ingrained conservatism of military ways ensured that any soldier who displayed original views or inventive tactics incurred the suspicion of madness. James Wolfe, the captor of Quebec, incurred just this suspicion and the Duke of Newcastle, opposing Wolfe's appointment to command the forces in Canada, complained that he was a madman. George II very justly replied: 'Mad, is he? Then I hope he will bite some of my other generals.'

No such hope was expressed of General Sir William Erskine (1770–1813). Twice confined to lunatic asylums, he was nonetheless appointed to be one of Wellington's commanders in the Peninsula. The Great Duke naturally had some misgivings, especially as Erskine's eyesight was so bad that he had to be pointed in the right direction to engage the enemy. Wellington cannot have been much comforted by this reassurance from the military secretary in London: 'No doubt he [Erskine] is a little mad at times, but he is lucid at intervals. I trust he will have no fit during the campaign, though I must say he looked a little mad as he embarked.'

He fulfilled all the Duke's misgivings by allowing a retreating French force to escape by pocketing an order and forgetting about it until too late. He later took his own life in Lisbon by jumping out of a window, and startled would-be rescuers by asking, 'Why on earth did I do that?' It may have been Erskine that Wellington had in mind when he said of some of his officers: 'I don't know about the French, but by God they frighten me.' (It has always disappointed me that Wellington said this in criticism of some of his officers, and not in praise of his rank and file infantry. In any case, I give the more famous version of this quotation. Another, fuller version is: 'As Lord Chesterfield said of the Generals of his day

"I only hope that when the enemy reads the list of their names, he trembles as I do."')

One officer who was unassailably a military genius but equally unassailably mad was Orde Charles Wingate (1903–44). The foundation of his military philosophy was the creation of small, mobile units, highly trained and specialised, operating behind enemy lines. An enthusiastic exponent of guerrilla warfare, he put these ideas into effect in the invasion of Abyssinia, in the creation of Force Gideon – a unit founded to defend Jewish settlements in Palestine, and above all in Burma where he raised and trained the Chindits – deep-penetration units to harass the Japanese forces behind the main battle areas.

But he also displayed characteristics that rarely find favour in officers' messes or in General Headquarters. Clothing was an issue with him. He disliked it, and went without it whenever possible. A passionate Zionist, as well as a stout Christian, he somewhat weakened his standing with the cause by interviewing Eliahu Elath, one of its leading lights, while completely unclothed. He conducted military briefings in the nude. He wore a garland of onions and garlic round his neck, and would frequently snack on them. He disliked bathing and instead would scrub himself with a toothbrush, often during meetings or briefings. He wore an alarm clock, some say on his wrist, some say in a finger ring. Even Winston Churchill, usually an admirer of irregular soldiers, decided that he was too erratic for high command. This may have been on the advice of his doctor, Lord Moran, who said 'Wingate seemed to me hardly sane – in medical jargon a borderline case. '

By no measure anywhere near Wingate as a tactician and leader, is the disagreeable figure of James Thomas Brudenell, seventh Earl of Cardigan. Dropped on his head as a child (he fell from his horse), he exhibited vanity and stupidity in equal proportions throughout his career. No one can deny that he had luck (and the troopers of the Light Brigade corresponding ill luck) when he was acquitted in an action for 'criminal conversation' (the Victorian euphemism for adultery) brought against him by Lord William Paget. Had Paget succeeded, Cardigan would certainly have been relieved of his commission, and would not therefore have been there to lead the Light Brigade, if lead is the word. (Paget had challenged Cardigan to a duel, but Cardigan declined to meet him.)

Cardigan again had luck at the Battle of Balaclava, during the episode of the Charge of the Light Brigade, charging right up to and through the Russian guns unscathed. The evidence that he then turned tail and bolted is mixed, and it must be remembered that the main witness against him (a much more redoubtable soldier), Lord George Paget, was a brother of Lord William Paget.

Cardigan's reason for refusing to meet Lord William

Paget is interesting. He had already, he said, been prosecuted for fighting a duel, and a second prosecution would be fatal to his career. He had indeed been prosecuted for grievously wounding a fellow officer in a duel in 1841. The prosecution failed on a ludicrous technicality. (It had not mentioned the word 'wounding' nor had it given the victim's full name.) But the prosecution demonstrated that Cardigan had used a rifled pistol with a hair trigger, thought unsportsmanlike at the time.

In spite of comic outbursts like his objection to a Moselle bottle on his mess table in the belief that it was a bottle of stout (the Black Bottle incident), Cardigan was really more silly and vicious than eccentric. One who was well up in the Wingate class was Lieutenant-Colonel Alfred Daniel Wintle, MC (1897–1966). He has already appeared in these pages because of his abiding affection for his umbrella (*see* pp. 5, 143), but umbrellas, really, were the least of it.

At the outbreak of war in 1914, although only sixteen, he 'irregularly attached himself' to an armoured-car squadron. Later, under shellfire, he admitted to being 'petrified'. His reaction was unconventional. He stood to attention and saluted until, in his own words, 'within 30 seconds I was able to become again an Englishman of action and carry out calmly the duties I had been trained to perform'. Englishness indeed was at the core of his being. When his father wanted to send him to school in Germany, he said: 'Attend a German school, sir? I would rather cut my hands off and blind myself in one eye. Only an English school is good enough for me.' As regards the eye, the Germans would oblige him later. Towards the end of his life he said: 'I get down on my knees every night and thank God for making me an Englishman. It is the greatest honour He could bestow. After all, he might have made me a chimpanzee, or a flea, a Frenchman or a German!'

I cannot speak for chimpanzees and fleas, but I doubt that the French or the Germans would have tolerated Colonel Wintle's career as happily as his fellow Englishmen. In 1917 he lost his left eye, a kneecap, and several fingers to a shell explosion, and his right eye was so damaged that he had to wear a monocle for the rest of his life. I am surprised that he hadn't thought of doing this anyway. The 'infernal quacks' invalided him home, but he tried to make a getaway from the military hospital by disguising himself as a nurse. Unfortunately the monocle gave him away. While in hospital he learnt from the nursing staff that Cedric Mays, a trooper in the Royal Dragoons, lay dying in the same hospital. The news brought out all the tender Florence Nightingale instincts lurking behind Wintle's crisp military façade. He marched into the ward and addressed the wounded man: 'Dying in bed is against King's Regulations,' he barked. 'Stop dying at once and when you get up, get your bloody hair cut.'

Trooper Mays recovered and lived to be ninety-five.

Wintle then wangled his way to the front with a warrant signed by a family friend. Almost at the war's end he won an MC for an episode in which, among much else, he single-handedly captured thirty-five German soldiers.

We can safely pass over the inter-war years, since, by his own admission, he found them 'intensely boring'. But he sprang into action again in 1939. At the age of forty-two he was not immediately considered for active service. 'It may have escaped your attention, but there is no fighting to be done in England,' he said and thought of resigning his commission and raising a private army. Instead he was employed in air intelligence work. In this capacity he devised a plan to rally the defeated French air forces and fly them to Britain to continue the fight. To achieve this he needed a plane himself, to get there. So he impersonated a superior officer, Air Commodore A. R. Boyle, and commandeered an aircraft. Prevented by Boyle in person, he threatened to shoot him saying, 'You and your kind should all be shot.' He was arrested and consigned to the Tower of London. En route to the tower his escorting officer lost his warrant, so Wintle originated and signed one himself, thus joining the elite ranks of officers who have placed themselves under arrest. Of his time in the Tower only his own words will do:

'My life in the Tower had begun. How different it

was from what I had expected. Officers at first cut me dead, thinking that I was some kind of traitor; but when news of my doings leaked out they could not do enough for me. My cell became the most popular meeting place in the garrison and I was as well cared for as if I had been at the Ritz. I would have a stroll in the (dry) moat after breakfast for exercise. Then sharp at eleven Guardsman McKie, detailed as my servant, would arrive from the officers' mess with a large whisky and ginger ale. He would find me already spick and span, for though I have a great regard for the Guards, they have not the gift to look after a cavalry officer's equipment. The morning would pass pleasantly. By noon visitors would begin to arrive. One or two always stayed to lunch. They always brought something with them. I remember one particularly succulent duck in aspic – it gave me indigestion – and a fine box of cigars brought by my family doctor. Tea time was elastic and informal. Visitors dropped in at intervals, usually bringing along bottles which were uncorked on the spot. I don't recall that any of them contained any tea. Dinner, on the other hand, was strictly formal. I dined sharp at eight and entertained only such guests as had been invited beforehand. After a few days of settling in, I was surprised to find that – as a way of life – being a prisoner in the Tower of London had its points.'

He was court-martialled, and, rather proud of having threatened Boyle with shooting, produced a list of other 'traitors' whom he considered worthy of the same treatment. The name Hore-Belisha, the then Secretary of State for War, figured on it.

He was released with a reprimand.

Possibly in an attempt to get rid of him, the authorities accepted his suggestion that he should be dropped into Occupied France. He was betrayed and arrested as soon as he landed, and imprisoned by the Vichy authorities. He warned his guards that it was his duty to escape, and then promptly did so, but was recaptured. He went on hunger strike on the unusual grounds that his guards were so badly turned-out that they were not fit to guard a British officer. They cleaned themselves up and consented to be inspected by him. He ceaselessly hectored his Vichy French guards about their cowardice and treachery to their country. He announced again his intention to escape, and successfully did so, making his way back to England via Spain. One is left prey to the suspicion that the French simply let him slip away. However, such was the impact of his dressings-down that the whole Vichy garrison of the prison, some 280 men, deserted and joined the Resistance.

Not content with military glory, the Colonel remained equally pugnacious after the war. Pausing only to commandeer a railway engine in protest against the lack of first-class carriages, he then stood for Parliament, losing handsomely, possibly because of his electioneering slogan: 'Guy Fawkes was the last man to enter Parliament with good intentions. You need another like me to carry on his good work.'

But he made legal history when he accused a solicitor named Nye of 'influencing' Wintle's elderly cousin into leaving her £44,000 estate to Nye. For reasons that are not immediately obvious, he chose to pursue his case by forcing Nye to remove his trousers and be photographed in this condition. Wintle was briefly imprisoned for this offence, but he pursued Nye for three years, eventually running out of money. He had therefore to present his case in the House of Lords himself. The Lords found in his favour, making him the first non-lawyer to win a case before them. He was also, I suspect, the first plaintiff to debag the defendant. His victory was no surprise to him:

'Not until I got to the Lords was I dealing with my intellectual equals.'

Like many another he enjoyed writing indignant letters to *The Times* – including one of a self-restraint rare indeed in Letters to the Editor:

Sir,
I have just written you a long letter. On reading it over, I have thrown it into the waste paper basket. Hoping this will meet with your approval,

I am, Sir,

Your obedient Servant,

and A. D. Wintle

It is important to remember that he achieved all the above while sporting a monocle and carrying a neatly furled umbrella.

Before moving on, I must add a reminiscence of my own. My grandfather, John Brooke Scrivenor, returning from Malaya at the outbreak of the war, felt that the Kaiser could not possibly be beaten without his help, in spite of his comparatively advanced age of thirty-eight. He was commissioned into the Royal Engineers, and late in 1914 he found himself maintaining telephone lines and other communications under constant shellfire just behind the front line. As dawn broke over a devastated landscape, he saw a dove-grey Rolls-Royce making its way over what was left of the road towards the front line. As it drew level, he stopped it. Inside was a uniformed chauffeur seated in a deluxe interior, with little silver holders for flowers and other ornaments. On the back seat was a large hamper.

'Where on earth do you think you're going? This is a battle area. They've been shelling this road all night.'

The chauffeur looked at him with all the disdain that the servants of the very rich reserve for the middle classes.

'I am taking his lordship his breakfast,' he said, as

if stating the most elementary and obvious of facts, and drove on. The car was not seen again.

At least, this is what I thought my grandfather did. I have recently been reminded by the fourth Lord Tweedsmuir that I heard this story years ago from his father, the third Lord Tweedsmuir, who told it about himself on an exercise in England in the Second War. My imagination had annexed the story and transposed it to my own family and France. I think the mud and the shellfire add a little something, so I shall stick with the revised version.

Strange though it seems to the unafflicted, there are men, quite a few, like Wintle, who actually enjoy battle. One such was Brigadier Peter Young, DSO, MC (1915–88), the Commando leader. The single entry 'MC' is misleading because Brigadier Young had an MC and two Bars – in effect he won the MC three times, as well as the DSO. I had the extraordinary privilege of knowing Peter Young, and once, with the impertinence of youth, I asked him why, since he was so brave, he had never won a VC. He looked at me with a countenance of the deepest woefulness and said: 'The big one, dear boy. It eluded me. *Jealousy in high places.*'

I cannot remember whether this was before or after he told me 'You can have a lot of fun in a battle with a Bren gun,' but it was certainly on another occasion, when we were lunching together, that he produced all his medals from a pocket, including many that I did not recognise, and spread them on the table.

'I got this one from King Hussein for driving off some Zionists who were trying to take over the Holy Mount in Jerusalem. I'm told the price of a taxi to Tel Aviv went up fiftyfold. I bet I'm the only British officer who has routed the Jews.'

An uneasy silence settled on the restaurant. To ease the situation I picked up one of the medals, so garish and grandiloquent that thoughts of the San Serafino Order of Purity and Truth (3rd Class) passed through my mind.

'No idea what that is,' he said. 'It arrived in the post three weeks ago. In the nick of time. I was suffering from medal starvation.'

In peacetime Peter Young founded the Sealed Knot, a society dedicated to restaging battles of the English Civil War. As its name suggests, the Sealed Knot had a bias towards the Royalist cause. The only time I attended a battle, it was one that had originally been a Roundhead victory. Peter shamelessly doctored the tactics, and the Royalists stormed home, victorious at all points.

Another such was Lieutenant-Colonel 'Jack' Churchill, DSO, MC (1906–96). He liked to go into battle variously armed with (a) a set of bagpipes, (b) a basket-hilted broadsword, and (c) a bow and arrow. He was, indeed, the last British soldier to kill an enemy with a longbow – a

German NCO in 1940 in a French village. It must have been the one eventuality for which the mighty Panzer divisions had not been trained. As for the sword, he said, 'In my opinion, sir, any officer who goes into action without his sword is improperly dressed.'

After much action in Norway and Italy – all involving pipes, sword and longbow – he was sent to support the partisans in Yugoslavia. Here he was captured, playing the pipes to the last, and sent first to Berlin and then to Sachsenhausen concentration camp. His captors assumed him to be related to Winston Churchill – which he was not – and dithered between using him in some political way and treating him harshly. He made two attempts to escape, the second one successful, as the war in Europe drew to a close. Anxious to miss no opportunities he got himself posted to the Far East, in the hope of action against the Japanese. To his bitter disappointment the Americans bombed Hiroshima and Nagasaki, ending the war before he got into action.

'If it wasn't for those damn Yanks,' he said, 'we could have kept the war going another ten years.'

In 1943, in Italy, he captured forty-two German soldiers, rather a large number to conduct to the rear. He explained how he managed it:

I always bring my prisoners back with their weapons;
it weighs them down. I just took their rifle bolts out
and put them in a sack, which one of the prisoners

carried. [They] also carried the mortar and all the bombs they could carry and also pulled a farm cart with five wounded in it... I maintain that, as long as you tell a German loudly and clearly what to do, if you are senior to him he will cry '*Jawohl*' and get on with it enthusiastically and efficiently whatever the... situation. That's why they make such marvellous soldiers.

These are twentieth-century men of action, forthright and exceedingly alarming. In earlier times it was possible to be an effective soldier and a fop at the same time. It is difficult to think of someone who could not pronounce his 'Rs' charging ashore with broadsword aloft while playing 'Hieland Laddie', but even if he didn't quite do this, Major-General Sir John Palmer Brabazon (1843–1922) was a highly effective officer, and certainly couldn't pronounce his 'Rs'.

He was tall, possessed of enviably good looks, of which he was somewhat vain, and known familiarly as 'beautiful Bwab'. His military career began in the Grenadier Guards, but he couldn't afford it and changed to a line regiment. Asked what regiment it was he replied: 'My dear fellow, I've a damn bad head for figures, so I can't wemember the number of the wegiment, but you take a twain fwom Waterloo to Aldershot and look about for a wegiment with gween facings.'

Ever the dandy, he sported a small tuft of hair under his lower lip, in addition to the resplendent moustaches above his upper lip. Technically this was a 'beard', forbidden to Regular officers in the British army. After a series of bitter exchanges with authority he was ordered to shave it off. He did, but also exactly one half of his moustache, giving him an electrifying appearance on parade.

This unlikely figure enjoyed a career of widespread active service – on General Roberts's famous march to Kandahar, in the Ashanti campaign, in the Sudan, and in the campaign mounted to relieve General Gordon at Khartoum. In this he repeatedly distinguished himself, and was wounded. At the outbreak of the Boer War he was given command of a cavalry force, at the age of fifty-six. There were whisperings that he was too old, and this nettled him. Standing on a hilltop with his staff he came under Boer rifle fire. He ordered his staff to take cover, but remained himself in the open, attracting heavy fire. When urged to take cover he said: 'I believe certain people have cast aspersions on my personal couwage; so I wish to show you all that my personal couwage is as good as ever it was.'

In the same campaign, despairing of the low standard of equipment for the British cavalry, he recommended 'shock' cavalry charges armed with tomahawks.

The painting in the National Portrait Gallery of 'Bwab's' near contemporary, Colonel Frederick

Gustavus Burnaby (1842–85), suggests another languid exquisite. He is shown lounging, his immensely long legs emphasised by his patrols, smoking a cigarette and looking supercilious. In fact Burnaby's record is that of daring man of action – almost a roughneck.

To start with he was the strongest man in the army. His party trick was to bend a poker round his or anyone else's neck. He encouraged his junior officers to hit him as hard as they could, in an attempt to hurt him. None succeeded. He once carried two small ponies – one under each arm – up and down the staircase of Windsor Castle. Queen Victoria's reaction is not recorded. Perhaps this is the occasion on which she said, 'We are not amused.' Campaigning for Parliament he once lifted two hecklers off their feet – one in each hand – to persuade them to be quiet. They were.

Among other adventurous activities, like ballooning, Burnaby undertook two journeys: a ride through the forbidden Russian conquests in Asia to the Khanate of Khiva; and a subsequent ride across Asia Minor from Scutari to Erzerum. He wrote best-selling books about both journeys. In 1884 he joined Sir Garnet Wolseley's 'Gordon Relief Expedition' (a description to which Gordon, while still alive, took grave exception), and at the Battle of El Teb he was involved in close hand-to-hand fighting with the Mahdi's forces. In obedience to the irregular soldier's preference for unusual weapons, he chose to fight the Sudanese with a double barrelled twelve-bore shotgun, employing the butt as well as the barrels to inflict damage on the enemy. Thus armed he rushed a superior body of enemy troops and ejected them from their defences.

The attempt to rescue Gordon had been mounted very unwillingly by the Liberal Prime Minister, Gladstone, who did not approve of imperial adventures. Since the expedition was, in that sense, their brainchild, his Liberal supporters in Parliament could not too strenuously object to it, but Fred Burnaby's exploits with a shotgun gave them their chance. For reasons scrutable only to the liberal mind, they deemed it outrageous to kill Mahdists with a shotgun instead of doing it with a Gatling gun, and Burnaby's conduct was the target of much criticism. He drew so much flak that the army authorities forbade him to continue with Wolseley's force. He ignored them, and was killed at the Battle of Abu Klea, again in hand-to-hand fighting, trying to rescue an isolated detachment outside the main square. In deference to liberal opinion he had left his shotgun behind. Abu Klea was the occasion when 'the fuzzy-wuzzies' famously 'broke a British Square', and Burnaby's death was the inspiration for Henry Newbolt's poem *Vitai Lampada*: 'the Gatling's jammed and the Colonel's dead' – I could go on – variously voted the best really bad poem and, by the unkind, the worst really bad poem, ever written. (In fact, it was a Gardner machine gun, not a Gatling, which jammed at Abu Klea.) William McGonagall also commemorated the battle in nineteen inimitable stanzas.

No account of military madness is complete without mentioning the British Army's performance in the Second Anglo-Boer War. This was Britain's Vietnam. Outclassed by a numerically inferior enemy, we resorted to inexcusable maltreatment of the civilian population. But it is with the army's follies rather than its brutalities that we are concerned here. Immediately the tall, commanding figure of Field Marshal Lord Methuen (1845–1932) springs to the forefront. Charged with relieving the siege of Kimberley he advanced against the Boer positions on the Modder River, disconcerted not to see them. 'They're not there,' he remarked. On cue, the Boers opened fire, not, as Methuen expected, from the high ground, but from trenches dug on the south side of the Modder River. Most of his division was trapped in the open and had no option but to lie down and wait. (Methuen's men had to do a lot of this.) The British artillery had a happy hour or so shelling the wrong targets, including their own side as a flank attack did eventually and feebly take shape. The Boers contained this too, but feeling themselves outnumbered, withdrew during the night to Magersfontein.

Again they dug themselves in at the base of the rising

ground. Methuen had an observation balloon, which would have revealed the Boer defences, but chose not to use it. (Compare this with Sir John French's refusal to take seriously reports by the Royal Flying Corps of the massing of von Kluck's First Army on the British front in 1914.) He ordered a night attack on the Boer positions by the Highland Brigade under Major-General Wauchope. Wauchope was given no time for proper reconnaissance. Again Methuen's artillery pounded the unoccupied hills, giving the Boers ample warning of the attack. The Highlanders advanced in massed quarter columns, over difficult terrain, in the dark, hindered by a violent thunderstorm. Some sources report General Wauchope muttering under his breath 'This is madness.' Before the brigade could deploy out of close order the Boers opened fire. Using modern Mauser bolt-action rifles, firing on a flat trajectory, their targets had little chance. Dawn found them pinned down in the open, where those that survived had to spend the remainder of a burning day. Among the first to be killed was General Wauchope, whose last words were recorded as 'Don't blame me for this, lads.'

Methuen himself was later captured by the Boers, generously treated by the Boer general Koos de la Rey, and returned to his own side. This in no way affected his strict impartiality when, later in the war, he was called upon to destroy the Boer settlement of Schweitzer-

Reneke, one of 30,000 Boer settlements destroyed by British forces in the war.

To conclude, here are the British in a more amiable light, not taking war too seriously.

'War is never a picnic, although of course soldiers do end up eating out of doors quite a lot.' Jesse Armstrong and Sam Bain, screenwriters.

'All the same, sir, I would put some of the colonies in your wife's name.' Joseph Hertz, British Chief Rabbi, speaking to George VI, 1940.

'Like everything the Germans do, it's frightfully good, but it goes on too long.' Evelyn Waugh, commenting on being under prolonged Stuka attack in Crete. This version was given to me by Brigadier Peter Young, who was with Waugh in the Commandos. A more general version is 'It was like German opera, too long and too loud'.

'My dear! The noise! The people!' Comment on Dunkirk by an unknown survivor, sometimes attributed to Brian Howard, the aesthete, although he was not at Dunkirk, but busily escaping from Occupied France by another route. (The story is also widely attributed to the actor Ernest Thesiger [*see* p. 115] commenting on the trenches of the First World War.)

'In defeat unbeatable; in victory unbearable.' Winston Churchill on Field Marshal Montgomery. And from the same source, on the subject of General de Gaulle: 'The greatest cross I have to bear is the Cross of Lorraine.'

'As he chased them away on his bike, he called them "oiks" –
in the circumstances surely the mildest of strictures.'

HONOURABLE MEMBERS
AND LEARNED FRIENDS

*'Hello. I'm your MP. Actually
I'm your candidate. Gosh!'*

Fate has robbed us of the opportunity to enjoy – for the first time in a long while – a genuinely entertaining prime minister. This role could have been filled to a nicety by Boris Johnson, and any amateur of British battiness must lament that he is out of the race. Anything can be expected from one whose third name is 'de Pleffel'. If his distracted, mad-professor manner is any indication, we have missed a treat. As the writer Bill Bryson has pointed out, 'interestingly wilful hair' is often a sign of genius, and Johnson is certainly blessed with interestingly wilful hair.

Boris Johnson has already substantially lightened our darkness. He read classics at Balliol, which is always a good start. He has a gift, similar to Prince Philip's, of saying provoking and controversial things. In 2009 he frivolously referred to the £250,000 paid to him each year by the *Daily Telegraph* for his column, as 'chickenfeed'. This offended practically everyone: other journalists who have never received more than £250 for similar endeavours; the employees of City Hall, where, as Mayor, Johnson was conducting a 'restructuring exercise' involving the loss of jobs; and everyone earning near or less than the national average wage, which at £25,000, is one-tenth of Johnson's fee for work which he candidly admitted he dashed off on Sunday evenings. In 2012 he condemned the London St Patrick's Day celebrations as 'Lefty Crap' after they were associated with Sinn Fein. On another occasion he is alleged to have said 'If you vote Conservative your wife will get bigger breasts' – a plainly jocular comment which caused much offence, and, anyway, where does it leave voters whose wives are already struggling with a size 44 D cup? He said of homosexual marriage that if two men marrying was OK, what about three, or even three men and a dog. His comments on Islamophobia made in the wake of the 7/7 bombings – later partly recanted – are well worth reading in their entirety. In brief, they add up to the assertion that Islamophobia is a natural and logical reaction to the writings of the

Koran, since they sanction the harsh and intolerant treatment of non-believers.

His capacity to offend against the current pieties is not confined to quotable 'gaffes'. After a Liverpool man, Kenneth Bigley, was executed by Islamic extremists in 2004, Johnson accused Liverpudlians of 'wallowing in vicarious victimhood' and mentioned the Hillsborough disaster as further evidence. Fatal. It is the modern equivalent of sacrilege to suggest any alternative to the view that the police were exclusively to blame. Johnson's suggestion was that 'drunken (Liverpool) fans at the back of the crowd . . . mindlessly tried to fight their way into the ground'. He was later reported as saying 'I am stunned at the hurt that this article has caused,' and subsequently visited Liverpool to apologise.

Also in 2004 he conducted an affair with Petronella Wyatt, which included passionate taxi rides during which the cabbie was asked to play discs of Wyatt herself singing Puccini. (It really annoys me that other people have done these things and I haven't. I wouldn't have the nerve to ask a London cabbie to do such a thing. 'Puccini? Woss 'e then? Italian? String 'em up, mate. It's the only language they understand.') In 2010 he was accused of failing to disclose a relationship with one Helen Macintyre, a City Hall adviser. In 2009 he rescued a young woman from mugging by a gang of other young women, one of them wielding an iron bar. As he chased them away on his bike, he called them 'oiks' – in the circumstances surely the mildest of strictures.

There is more, but this is enough to provoke lifelong regret that it was Mr Mitchell, and not Mr Johnson, who propelled his bicycle through the wrong gates in Downing Street. Had it been Johnson, 'Plebgate' would surely have been the least of it.

Members of Parliament in general, while frequently venal, vulgar and venomous – and idle, ignorant and ignominious into the bargain – are very rarely mad on the grand scale. That is not to say that the lower house has not harboured some wits. It has, but their wit is more pointed than errant. So before we look at the heavyweights in the other place, we'll see what fun we can wring out of the junior school.

We will start with one whose main fame as a parliamentarian lies in his having so often been turned out of Parliament – John Wilkes. Wilkes was one of those politicians who arrive at radicalism through a sort of disappointed patriotic Toryism. In any case he was radical enough seriously to annoy the Whig establishment, to which he added a reputation as a rake. It was he who released a baboon, disguised as the devil, among the inebriated 'worshippers' at the Hellfire Club. Among those made to look ridiculous by this was the fourth Earl of Sandwich, and as a result one of those thunderous eighteenth-century exchanges is alleged to have taken place:

> Sandwich: ''Pon my soul, Wilkes, I don't know whether you'll die on the gallows or of the pox.'
> Wilkes: 'That depends, my Lord, whether I first embrace your Lordship's principles, or your Lordship's mistresses.'

If you think Wilkes's retort is a bit too pat and polished, you may be right. The exchange has also been ascribed to Honoré Gabriel Riqueti, Comte de Mirabeau and Cardinal Jean-Sifrein Maury, and it does indeed have a French ring to it. It gains a certain something by having a priest – and a cardinal to boot – as one of the speakers. But Wilkes deserves his reputation for repartee. He was once told by a constituent that he 'would rather vote for the devil'. Wilkes replied: 'Naturally. And if your friend decides against standing, can I count on your vote?'

A whole book could be filled, and many have, with Sir Winston Churchill's wisecracks, one-liners and retorts. Genuine wits, by which I mean people who take a droll relish in the errant and sometimes contradictory power of words, do not often attain high office. Falsehood and self-importance – the two essentials of worldly success – cannot keep their heads above the waters of humour and irony. Perhaps the only two genuine wits to have risen right to the top in modern times are Abraham Lincoln and Winston Churchill. Churchill's repartee is well-documented and very famous, and I will give only a few examples.

For much of his career Churchill was deeply unpopular. An MP called Paling once rose to his feet and denounced Churchill as a 'dirty dog'. Churchill replied: 'If the honourable member will step outside, I will show him what a dirty dog can do to a paling.' Irritated beyond control by something Churchill had said, Nancy Astor once shouted at him: 'If I were your wife I would put poison in your coffee'. 'And if I were your husband I would drink it.' (This exchange is sometimes attributed to Nancy Astor and F. E. Smith.) Still less gallantly, when accused by the Labour MP, Bessie Braddock, of being drunk, he replied: 'And you, madam, are ugly, but tomorrow I'll be sober'.

These are famous remarks, repeated in many anthologies. Here are a few less well-known specimens of Churchilliana, which seem to me to demonstrate his love of words and their power:

'This report, by its very length, defends itself against the risk of being read.'

'We contend that for a nation to try to tax itself into prosperity is like a man standing in a bucket and trying to lift himself up by the handle.'

'Men occasionally stumble over the truth, but most of

them pick themselves up and hurry off as if nothing ever happened.'

'A fanatic is one who can't change his mind and won't change the subject.'

'An appeaser is one who feeds a crocodile, hoping it will eat him last.'

And a last little *tour de force* about English grammar and the Preposition:

'What made you pick this book I didn't want to be read to out of up for?'

He did not always have it his own way. Sir Stafford Cripps, a man of such high-minded rectitude that Churchill said of him 'There but for the grace of God goes God', once took Churchill to task for high-handed behaviour. Churchill defended himself:

'I am the humble servant of the Lord Jesus Christ and of the House of Commons.'

'I hope you treat Jesus better than you treat the House of Commons,' Cripps replied.

Even Churchill's famous powers of oratory came in for comment:

'He has devoted the best years of his life to preparing his impromptu speeches.' – F. E. Smith.

Another with pretensions to wit – albeit very acid wit – to reach prime ministerial rank was the Duke of Wellington. His military career did not really prepare him for the horrid realities of cabinet government.

His first cabinet meeting as Prime Minister left him nonplussed:

'An extraordinary affair. I gave them their orders and they wanted to stay and discuss them.'

Politicians naturally attract each other's censure:

'Lloyd George did not seem to care which way he travelled providing he was in the driver's seat.'– Lord Beaverbrook.

'That's the trouble with Anthony [Eden] – half mad baronet, half beautiful woman.' — R. A. Butler, Tory politician.

'Like being savaged by a dead sheep.'– Denis Healey on being attacked in a speech by Geoffrey Howe.

And although no politician, Margot Asquith neatly impaled Lloyd George:

'He can't see a belt without hitting below it.'

Sometimes they are honest about themselves and their calling.

'There are no true friends in politics. We are all sharks circling and waiting for traces of blood to appear in the water.' – Alan Clark, Tory MP.

'If you want to succeed in politics you must keep your conscience well under control.'– David Lloyd George.

'You don't tell deliberate lies, but sometimes you have to be evasive.' – Margaret Thatcher.

The House of Lords presents a very different picture. Before the exclusion of hereditary peers it often demonstrated very high standards of waywardness and peculiarity. John Conrad Russell, fourth Earl Russell (1921–1987) was the eldest son of the philosopher and mathematician. He was educated at his father's experimental school where there were no formal lessons and the pupils were encouraged to contradict their teachers and answer back. He was later educated at Harvard. Both these influences may have been present when in 1978 he addressed the House of Lords in a speech so strange that it became the only speech in the history of Parliament that Hansard did not record. In it he advocated the abolition of law and order, universal leisure for all, and some means of preventing the police from raping young people and putting them in brothels. Girls should be given their own house at the age of twelve, and three-quarters of the national wealth should be given to them so that marriage would become unnecessary and a girl could have as many husbands as she wanted. The whole speech led with forcible logic to its inexorable conclusion – that Leonid Brezhnev and Jimmy Carter were in fact the same person.

Not long after this he was diagnosed with schizophrenia, and thus became the only person in Britain to be denied the vote on two grounds – being a peer, and being insane.

Stuff like this must at least have kept their Lordships awake. Sleep is a constant theme in memoirs of the red benches. The eighth Duke of Devonshire, whom we have already met as Lord Hartington, shooting low pheasants, killing a dog and peppering the spectators, was particularly prone to profound slumbers. He was once seen asleep in the House of Lords and when woken he looked at the clock and said: 'Good Heavens, what a bore. I shan't be in bed for another seven hours.' Even more remarkably, when asked why he so rarely spoke in the House he replied: 'I can't refrain from yawning in the middle of my rare orations. Indeed I fell asleep one afternoon and dreamt that I was addressing that just assembly when someone woke me up, and by Jove I was!'

Sentiments echoed by the seventh Earl of Onslow (1938–2011). In many ways a reformer, in others he remained what we expect from an hereditary member of the Upper House. He opposed all reform in the Church of England, announcing stoutly: 'One hundred years ago, the Church was in favour of fox hunting and against buggery. Now it is in favour of buggery and against fox hunting.' Of reforming the House of Lords, which he to some extent supported, he said: 'I will be sad if I either look up or down after my death and don't see my son fast asleep on the same benches on which I have slept.'

Judges too sometimes nod off. In the 1990s a Crown Court judge was accused by the prosecuting barrister of being asleep during the presentation of the prosecution's case.

'I was not asleep.'

'With respect, I distinctly heard your lordship snoring.'

'I was not snoring. That was my springer spaniel.'

'With respect, m'lud, it is just as bad that your spaniel should be snoring during the presentation of evidence.'

'He was not snoring, and I shall not have you say that he was. He suffers from asthma.'

Let us hope it was the same judge who appealed plaintively to a barrister who had made a topical reference that the judge did not understand:

'Will learned counsel please explain? What are Diana Doors?'

Like clergymen, judges used to be very difficult to remove, and this gave them the security to develop marked idiosyncrasies. Sir Harry Vaisey (1877–1965) was a senior judge in the Chancery Division. He is chiefly remembered for ruling that a Christian name cannot be altered without an Act of Parliament, and that a will is invalid if such a name has been changed without an Act of Parliament. The ruling is universally ignored, but if you wish to change your name, the deed must still contain the caveat: 'Notwithstanding the decision of Mr Justice Vaisey *in re Parrott, Cox v Parrott*, the applicant wishes the enrolment to proceed'. There is something very glorious in the thought of Mr Cox and Mr Parrott battling out such a tiny point. Mr Justice Vaisey is also remembered for colourful asides from the bench: 'It is a fearful thing to contemplate that when you are driving along the road, a heavy horse may at any moment drop from the sky on top of you.'

Towards the end of his career his eyesight and hearing became very bad. He relied on the clerk of the court to pass up to him digests – in large capital letters – of what was said in court. His judgments got better and better.

I must declare an interest. Mr Justice Vaisey was my great-uncle. Family myth credits him with the following *obiter dictum*, made during a divorce hearing: 'Any man who wears a bow tie declares himself to be an adulterer.'

Tradition insists that all *obiter dicta* should be in some way ridiculous, but judges frequently score points off defendants, witnesses and counsel. Lord Birkett is credited with this exchange:

Prisoner: 'As God is my judge, I'm innocent.'

Birkett: 'He isn't, I am, and you're not!'

And a prisoner appearing before Mr Justice Darling took objection to being called a professional criminal, offering this extenuation: 'I've only done two jobs, and each time I've been nabbed.'

'It has never been suggested that you are successful in your profession.'

Things got tougher under Judge Michael Argyle (1915–1999). An ex-heavyweight boxer and sporting enthusiast, he used throughout his career to pop out during recess to the nearest betting shop. He was certainly the only Old Bailey judge to keep whippets for racing. His sentencing policy was erratic, but there was some method in his madness. He was harsh in cases where he thought the accused was an unreformable professional criminal, and lenient elsewhere. What raised the blood pressure of everyone to the left of Genghis Khan were his off-the-cuff comments:

To a man charged with attempted rape, imposing a suspended sentence: 'You come from Derby which is my part of the world. Off you go and don't come back.'

To a policewoman giving evidence: 'You are far too attractive to be a policewoman – you should be a film star.'

To the victim of a mugging: '[You are] a vicious little sodomite from Glasgow.'

And, when a strike had cancelled television coverage of a Test Match: 'It is enough to make an orthodox Jew want to join the Nazi Party.'

He is credited with coining the term 'Thiefrow' to describe London Airport.

An even more cavalier attitude to sentencing was taken by Sir Melford Stevenson (1902–87). Few would cavil at his sending down the Kray brothers for thirty years, but giving a variety of sentences including jail, borstal and deportation to eight Cambridge 'students' in the wake of the Garden House riot was criticised as excessive. During the Kray trial Stevenson conceded that Ronnie

Kray had spoken the truth twice – once when he called the prosecuting counsel a 'fat slob', and once when he said that the judge was biased. Like Argyll, his off-the-cuff remarks caused frequent outrage:

Of a plaintiff in a divorce case: 'He chose to live in Manchester, a wholly incomprehensible choice for any free man to make.'

To a man accused of rape: 'I see you come from Slough. It is a terrible place. You can go back there.'

And best of all, on passing sentence: 'I must confess I cannot tell whether you are innocent or guilty. I am giving you three years. If you are guilty you have got off lightly, if innocent let this be a lesson to you.'

With judges like these on the loose, small wonder that barristers occasionally give way to impatience, and this section shall be the exclusive territory of F. E. Smith, first Earl of Birkenhead (1872–1930). There is much to be said about Smith – his brilliant public career, his heavy drinking and high living, his friendship with Churchill – but he was also the man who has been ruder to judges than anyone else before or since – and often with lethal point and accuracy. It seems simplest just to list his triumphs:

Judge: 'You are extremely offensive, young man!'

Smith: 'As a matter of fact we both are; and the only difference between us is that I am trying to be, and you can't help it.'

Judge: 'What do you suppose I am on the bench for?'

Smith: 'It is not for me, Your Honour, to attempt to fathom the inscrutable workings of Providence.'

Judge: 'I have read your case, Mr Smith, and I am none the wiser now than I was when I started.'

Smith: 'None the wiser perhaps, my lord, but certainly better informed.'

Master of the Rolls: 'Really, Mr Smith, do give this court credit for some little intelligence.'

Smith: 'That is the mistake I made in the court below, my lord.'

And lastly, one in which Smith unquestionably set up his victim for the knock-out blow . . .

Smith: 'At the time my client was as drunk as a judge.'

Judge: 'Mr Smith. I think you will find that the phrase is "as drunk as a lord".'

Smith: 'As your lordship pleases.'

'Unfortunately, as he sped forward, the
rope snapped, and Horace (I'm afraid no
other word exists) was catapulted into the
Murphy picnic basket.'

NEARER MY GOD TO THEE: GOD AND THE ESTABLISHMENT

*'Like an Archangel, ecstatically announcing the
millennium, only to discover that it clashes
unpardonably with Henley.' – Saki*

In the context of this book 'religion' can mean only
one thing – the Anglican Church. This august body
once boasted great glories – the Book of Common Prayer,
the King James Bible, all the magnificent buildings we
pinched from the Catholics, and, among much else, the
Parson's Freehold, a device to protect the parochial clergy
from interference by bishops, or indeed politicians. The
Parson's Freehold made it very difficult to remove a
vicar from his living, and clergymen therefore had the
latitude to develop extreme irregularities of behaviour.
This made possible the church's greatest glory of all –
the career of the Reverend Harold Davidson, the Rector
of Stiffkey in Norfolk.

Even without the court hearing in 1932 that made him

world famous, Harold Davidson has two unassailable claims to immortality. He was the only clerk in holy orders ever to be arrested by the Naval Police in a brothel in Cairo, and he was the last Christian to be eaten by lions. He was also thrown out of a nudist camp in Yorkshire, and preached from a barrel on Blackpool's Golden Mile.

It happened in the following way.

The Rector of Stiffkey's main, possibly sole, pre-occupation was girls. Any girls would do – any number of them – but fallen girls were best. If they hadn't fallen already, the Rector was quite happy to help them. Throughout his time as the Rector of Stiffkey he would leave after Matins on Sunday (or at the very latest on Monday morning) and return on the following Saturday – often as late as Sunday morning, too late for Matins. The intervening time was spent in London, pursuing his calling as 'the prostitute's padre'. And girls. Lots of girls. Tea shops – from which he was regularly banned – were his favourite beat because of the ready availability of waitresses. He later claimed to have 'saved' over 1,000 women from falling.

But in 1920 he met a girl who had fallen so far that it took ten years to save her. She was Rose Ellis, twenty years old, and a prostitute. Saving her involved paying her rent, taking her on a trip to Paris, and allowing her to lance a boil on his buttock. However, in spite of her greater years, she had not managed to fall as far as Barbara Harris, sixteen, also a prostitute, whom the Rector met in 1930. Acting in unknowing confederacy with the Rector's churchwarden, Major Philip Hamond (a Boer War veteran), these two girls brought about the Rector's downfall.

In 1931 Major Hamond complained to the Bishop of Norwich about (a) the Rector's patchy attention to parish matters, (b) the presence of young women at the rectory (young women of such a type that the villagers sometimes came across copulating couples in the hedgerows), and (c) the Rector's failure to attend an Armistice Day service. The Bishop hired private detectives to investigate the truth of these complaints. They found Rose Ellis. Piqued by the Rector's interest in a younger woman, and primed with glasses of port by the Bishop's detectives, Rose Ellis Told All.

The press, possibly tipped off by the Bishop's legal adviser, published the story on 1 February 1932, and it immediately made headlines. The Rector protested his innocence – from his pulpit. Trippers flocked to Stiffkey on Sundays and cheered him to the echo. But then Barbara Harris, who had not known about Rose, also succumbed to pique. She wrote to the Bishop of Norwich accusing the Rector of rape, a breach of promise, and much else.

Nineteen-thirty-two was not the year to be the

Bishop of Norwich. He convened a Consistory Court to try the Rector for a number of offences including adultery with Rose Ellis and associating with women of loose character. The Rector denied the charges. The ensuing hearing, instead of being over in a week, ran for five months, from March to July 1932. On almost every day of those months the case made headlines, as a bewildering array of landladies, waitresses, and circus performers processed through the witness box testifying to the Rector's strange perambulating lifestyle, roving about London accosting girls. In due course the prosecution produced a photograph of the Rector with a naked woman. He protested that 'a titled lady' had invited him to tea and had surprised him by appearing naked. His 'titled lady' turned out to be Estelle Douglas, fifteen years old, to whom the Rector had suggested that he could advance her career as a swimwear model. He again protested that he had been tricked and that he had assumed the photograph to be for swimwear modelling purposes. Estelle was the daughter of one of his oldest friends.

Throughout the hearing the Rector remained the incumbent of Stiffkey, with a perfect right to preach there. On 2 June, in an attempt to silence the media circus besieging the vicarage and the church, Major Hamond put in a pinch-hitter, the Reverend R .H. Cattell, to take evensong in the Rector's place. The

Rector appeared, and a brisk tug-of-war developed for the possession of the church's Bible. The Rector won.

It was his last victory. On 8 July the Consistory Court found him guilty of the charges against him, and referred sentencing to the Bishop of Norwich.

Foremost in the Rector's mind was the need to clear his name. Scorning the normal channels, he at once took to the stage, signing up in a series of variety acts, both in London and the provinces. He drew big houses, but theatrical managers, possibly leant on by authority, suddenly ceased to sign him. Never at a loss, the Rector took to living in a barrel on Blackpool's Golden Mile, sandwiched between Mariana the Gorilla Girl, the Bearded Lady from Russia and the Fattest Man in the World. He was permitted to hold one last service at Stiffkey, but as he left Major Hamond kicked him severely in the posterior – an offence for which the Major was later fined. The Rector was formally defrocked on 21 October 1932.

For four years he stuck it out in his barrel, protesting his innocence. But he could not entirely abandon his pastoral mission, and in 1936 he was fined for 'pestering' two sixteen-year-old girls at Victoria Station.

However, to the Rector, Blackpool had always seemed a bit *déclassé* for one who had been at Oxford. He was therefore glad to sign up with 'Captain' Freddie Rye, whose animal show was based in Skegness. The distinction is not immediately clear to me, but it satisfied the Rector. Under the Captain's watchful eye, the Rector was able to preach sermons outside a cage containing two lions – Freddie and Toto. After the sermon he briefly entered the cage – a conscious echo of Daniel in the Lions' Den.

On 28 July 1937, he preached as usual to a large crowd. Afterwards he entered the cage. For reasons at which we can only guess, he flourished a whip, cracked it and shouted – something Daniel would never have done. Toto took it in good part, but Freddie appeared greatly vexed. He seized the Rector's head and shoulder in his jaws and dragged him round the cage, inflicting injuries from which the Rector never recovered, in spite of heroic attempts to save him on the part of the lion's tamer – sixteen-year-old Irene Somner.

Few have risen to these heights, but Harold Davidson is far from being alone. When I referred to the Anglican Church as 'august', it was not merely a piece of hyperbole. In what other jurisdiction could a citizen enjoy the privilege of being shot by an archbishop? This fate was experienced in July 1621, when Peter Hawkins, gamekeeper to Lord Zouch, was shot dead with a bow and arrow by George Abbott, the then Archbishop of Canterbury, a prelate notorious for his savage punishment of any form of heresy or non-conformism. So far as was known the keeper was neither a Nonconformist nor a heretic, and the Archbishop's action was seen as being a little over the top. Except by the King, James VI and I, who pardoned him.

Similarly, where else could a serious gangster be acquitted on the perjured evidence of a clergyman? This was the good fortune of Jack Spot, accused of a knife attack on another gangster, Albert Dimes, in London in 1955. The Reverend Basil Andrews, aged eighty-eight, testified that Dimes was the assailant. Ultimately it did Spot little good. It was discovered that Spot's friend, Moishe 'Blue Boy' Goldstein, had paid Andrews to provide false witness, an offer readily accepted because the clergyman owed many debts at race tracks and in gambling clubs. The judge asked Andrews, 'Do you ever speak the truth?', to which Andrews replied 'No' – a baffling response on which philosophers have expended torrents of ink, but which in the best traditions of the English bench the judge passed lightly over.

And what about the Reverend Sir Henry Bate Dudley, Bt (also known as Reverend Henry Bate) who, in addition to numerous fist fights, fought five duels, did time for libelling the Duke of Richmond, and wrote comic opera scripts? Or the unhappy Dr Dodd who, in June 1777, was executed for forgery? And the Reverend Edward Drax Free who, charged with fornication, drunkenness, lewdness, assault and keeping pigs in the churchyard, barricaded himself in his rectory, precipitating an armed siege? Or the Reverend William Jackson, who trumped up charges of sodomy against his opponents, engaged in espionage on behalf of the French, and committed suicide in the dock?

As if all this were not enough, what other Church can boast a senior archbishop who was also a pirate? Lancelot Blackburne, who became Archbishop of York in 1724, had in his youth been a pirate in the Caribbean. Later, commenting on his episcopacy, the writer Horace Walpole said 'he retained nothing of his former profession but his seraglio'. His fondness for women in no way impeded his career in the Church. While Dean of Exeter he had a secret tunnel constructed so that he could visit his neighbour, Mrs Martyr, clandestinely. He paid little attention to his ecclesiastical duties, preferring to spend his time, like Harold Davidson, in London. A scurrilous poem of the time credited him with a taste for two girls at a time – a sort of archiepiscopal sandwich. It was also rumoured that he employed the famous highwayman, Dick Turpin, as his butler.

With the morals of the nation entrusted to this very diverse body, the British Establishment has always enjoyed an equivocal relationship with it. Even that bedrock of the Anglican faith, the stupendous Authorised Version of the Bible, has incurred doubt, if not actual censure, in the highest circles. 'A wonderful book, but there are some very queer things in it,' remarked King George V. And so there are. 'Deep calleth unto deep at the noise of thy waterspouts.' Possibly he took this to be a comment on the plumbing at Balmoral.

Another voice, equally resounding in its way, expressed a very common misgiving about the Bible. 'I read the Book of Job last night. I don't think God comes very well out of it,' wrote Virginia Woolf to Lady Robert Cecil in 1922. And another, more robust, judgement echoes the same opinion. 'God! Isn't God a shit!' exclaimed Randolph Churchill at regular intervals, when, in an effort to stop him talking, Evelyn Waugh bet him that he could not read the Bible at a sitting.

There is indeed, a feeling that God, and all the attendant doctrine, is merely a regrettable necessity. The Church is really there to provide preferment for younger sons, or to represent, as used to be said, the Tory Party at prayer. 'Merit!' expostulated Lord Westmorland in 1835. 'We have come to a pretty pass if they talk of *merit* for a bishopric.' His contemporary, Lord Melbourne, used almost the same words. 'Things have come to a pretty pass when religion is allowed to invade the sphere of private life.' As late as 1962 the writer J. B. Priestley was able to remark 'It is hard to tell where the MCC ends and the Church of England begins'. And, although a fiction, the playwright Peter Barnes's character (in *The Ruling Class*), Lord Gurney, gives a proof of the existence of God that must have occurred to many a grandee. 'When I pray to Him, I find I'm talking to myself.' Even Bertrand Russell was not entirely free of this sort of egotheism. 'The Chinese said they would build a shrine to my memory. I have some slight regret that this did not happen as I might have become a God, which would have been very *chic* for an atheist.'

All in all there has often been an air among the highest in the land of plain snootiness with regard to the Church and its appointments, and this persists. Commenting, in 2013, on Richard Chartres, Bishop of London, Giles Fraser, an Anglican clergyman, called him 'the sort of bishop you would get if you went to Harrods'. I can remember when you could buy black panthers in the Pet Department at Harrods, and if their Bishops & Sundry Clergy Department is conducted on the same spacious principles I cannot see what the objection is.

Finally, if you think I have neglected other faiths, snootiness is not lacking there, either. Here is Randolph Churchill again, addressing the Pope. 'I expect you know my friend Evelyn Waugh, who, like your holiness, is a Roman Catholic.'

Did he treat the Pope to his opinion of God? History is silent on the point.

The Anglican Church has lost much of its magnificence since it abandoned the Book of Common Prayer and the Authorised Version. But it is good to note that some of the old spirit lingers – even to the extent of performing miracles. This was the achievement of the vicar of the Church of St John with St Michael in Bournemouth. In 1995 one of his parishioners, Mrs Brenda Murphy, was enjoying a picnic on her lawn with her young daughter.

'Mummy,' said the little girl, 'I would like a pet cat.'

Mrs Murphy did not want to commit herself just at that moment, so she said: 'In that case, let us pray for one.' And down on their knees they went.

But hardly had the first 'Our Father' passed their lips, than a cat, screeching loudly, came hurtling through the air, and fell into their picnic basket. Picture Mrs Murphy's predicament. She could hardly blast her daughter's dramatically reinforced faith by offering some secular explanation, and anyway, what explanation was there? So pocketing both cat and conscience, she withdrew indoors – her daughter clutching her new pet cat with obvious devotion.

But she remained troubled in her conscience, and when, a few days later, she met the vicar in the supermarket, she opened her heart to him. The vicar's face clouded over, but more it seemed with annoyance than with theological perplexity.

'Is it a black and white cat?' he asked. Mrs Murphy admitted that it was, and the vicar was able to identify it as his own cat, Horace.

What had happened was this. On the day of the picnic,

Horace had got stuck up a tall but slender sapling. Unable to reach him, the vicar had tied one end of a rope to the tree, as high up as possible, and the other end to his car, in an attempt the bend the tree low enough to reach Horace. Unfortunately, as he sped forward, the rope snapped, and Horace (I'm afraid no other word exists) was catapulted into the Murphy picnic basket.

'The Lord moves in mysterious ways indeed,' said the vicar.

I hope they made him a bishop.

'As the waters closed over the vessel's hull the Princess turned to her companion and said quietly "I shall be very disappointed if George doesn't come up again."'

'BUGGER BOGNOR!' WAYWARD ROYAL BEHAVIOUR

'My Lord, we had forgot the fart.'

Where the Higher Lunacy is concerned, royalty are often a disappointment. Monarchs are constrained by their position in a way that the merely rich and privileged are not. They have to *do* something, often fatal to the full development of eccentricity. They must also, in public at any rate, guard their tongues for constitutional reasons. They are, in short, running under a handicap, and if they fail to reach the dizzying heights of battiness achieved by some of their peers and subjects, they are not to be blamed. They have more important things to see to, and, besides, they have done their best.

We must leave aside those who actually were mad,

like Henry VI and poor George III (although surely addressing an oak tree as the King of Prussia was conscious satire?).Over the years our monarchs have not been strong on jokes – at least not in public – but apart from this they have managed quite uncannily to reflect the general tenor of the majority of their subjects.

To start with they have often displayed a very British philistinism and suspicion of the arts, in spite of owning some of the best pictures and other artefacts in the country. The remark made by the Emperor Joseph to Mozart – 'Too many notes, my dear Mozart' – is possibly apocryphal. In the same vein the Duke of Gloucester (or the Duke of Cumberland, or George III; it hardly matters) is alleged to have said – 'Another damned, thick, square book! Always scribble, scribble, scribble! Eh! Mr Gibbon?' But while the Emperor Joseph's remark is a species of sacrilege, anyone who has actually tried to read *The History of the Decline and Fall of the Roman Empire* must have some sympathy for whichever British Royal had a go at Gibbon.

This was perhaps an unsolicited remark, but royalty are often propelled by their duties into situations where they must comment and/or be damned – often on matters in which they have no personal interest. King George VI once attended an exhibition of the paintings of the modernist John Piper, whose work tended to the sombre. After looking in silence at the pictures – many of them landscapes – the King said: 'Pity you had such bloody awful weather'.

Are such apparently naïve comments in fact deliberate irony – both self-deprecating and quietly putting down the subject? Or maybe outright jokes? Said with sufficient humour one can imagine both the King and John Piper laughing. We shall never know. And was the present Prince of Wales joking when he wrote asking his publisher for a royalty statement? Surely yes, or at the very least he must have been conscious of an enjoyable irony. His grandmother, however, shared her husband's inability to take modernism seriously. 'Osbert was wonderful, as you would expect, and Edith of course, but then we had this rather lugubrious man in a suit, and he read a poem . . . I think it was called The Desert. And first the girls got the giggles and then I did and then even the King.'

During the war, Osbert Sitwell, perhaps more patriotically than wisely, assembled a gaggle of intellectuals to entertain the King and Queen and their daughters at Windsor – a sort of Royal Command Variety Act of highbrows. T. S. Eliot read *The Waste Land* – certainly wasted in this instance. It is understandable enough to giggle at T. S. Eliot, but to do so without simultaneously giggling at Edith Sitwell is surely perverse. Perhaps it was just comedy overload. All comics need a warm-up act, and Edith Sitwell merely softened the royals up for Tom Eliot's well-known knock-about routine.

Likewise Prince Philip, the Duke of Edinburgh, in 1969 – a little in advance of his true vintage years as a dropper of well-merited bricks: 'I declare this thing open – whatever it is.'

'It' was the extension to the Vancouver City Hall, designed by Townley and Matheson, a company at whose door responsibility for much of the appearance of Vancouver may be laid. Pictures reveal, certainly a boring and uninspired structure, but not an outrageous example of modernism in the full meaning of the act. But the Duke was right. 'Function' is not immediately evident in 'form', and my own guess would be the premises of an expensive veterinary practice, or a well-heeled primary school.

Have you ever played Lady Macbeth? I thought not. Neither have I. But if you have, and feel you have done so well, you expect comments after the performance that at least touch in some way on the character and her place in the tragedy: her steely determination; how, having had to encourage him, her husband's ruthlessness then outstrips hers; the ultimate tragedy of her madness. But in 1937 the actress Judith Anderson was presented to Queen Mary (wife of George V) after her performance of Lady Macbeth, to be greeted with the following, obviously heartfelt, comment. 'I really *felt* for you in the scene in which you tried to make the party go.'

Well, yes. Nothing wrecks the plans of a hostess more than the ghost of a man her husband has murdered turning up, shaking its gory locks. It is possible however that Queen Mary had read the character more closely than you might suppose. When Lady Macbeth is told that her 'royal master's murdered' – which she already knows perfectly well, of course – she replies 'What! In our house?' a very suburban reaction for a Thane's wife in a freezing Scottish castle, suddenly apprised that the head of state has been bopped off in the spare room.

A brief digression on Queen Mary herself is not out of place. She was a formidable figure. Described by the diarist Chips Channon as 'looking like the Jungfrau, white and sparkling in the sun', she was an object of dread in the houses she visited. At the conclusion of the visit the hosts would often be approached by an aide, who would say 'We very much liked the Chinese Chippendale commode in our bedroom', upon which the poor wretches were expected to hand it over. She met her match in Lord Kitchener, who was told, 'We particularly admired the Persian sword above the fireplace.' He replied that he had always admired the Ming vase in Her Majesty's hallway at Sandringham. Protracted negotiations took place, lasting years, and when both parties eventually received their 'presents', each found that they had been given an obvious copy.

Queen Mary experienced much anguish as a result of her son's affair with Wallis Simpson, and when he eventually abdicated to marry Simpson she remarked: 'Really, this might be Rumania' – a most unjust remark, since it took a world war to persuade King Carol II of Romania to abdicate, not merely the allurements of an American divorcee. And indeed there was something petulant and weedy in the way Edward VIII gave it all up so limply. Was it really necessary to marry the woman? These pages are littered with examples of the mistresses of the mighty, who seem to have a high old time. Couldn't she just have stuck around as his moll? And his abdication address, with its repeated emphasis on the first person singular – not the stiff upper lip as we know it. Where royal declarations are concerned it cannot begin to compare with 'Bugger Bognor' (see below).

As comments on the abdication went, Queen Mary's reaction was dignity itself. Compare the enraged splutterings of an unnamed naval officer: 'It is not seemly that an Admiral of the Fleet should become the Third Mate of an American tramp.'

It is necessary to stay with Queen Mary for a moment. When she and her husband were Prince and Princess of Wales, they visited the fleet at Portsmouth, where Admiral Jacky Fisher persuaded the prince to go down in a submarine – then very much a novelty. As the waters closed over the vessel's hull the Princess turned to her companion and said quietly 'I shall be very disappointed if George doesn't come up again'.

Like many royal sayings, at first sight this seems bland to the point of banality, but it is really a rather remarkable utterance. Is it merely an example of British understatement, or is there some hidden message, some little barb concealed in it? If taken literally, it is hardly the comment of a wife who cares very greatly if her husband does surface again, but is it intended to be taken literally? The horrid suspicion begins to dawn – is it a joke? Was Queen Mary expecting her ladies-in-waiting to roll around on the dock, clutching their sides?

The public face of royalty discourages joking. But this doesn't mean that they never joke. I suspect that they joke a great deal. They are in a unique position to develop private jokes that can pass almost unnoticed by anyone but themselves. In any case there is a long record of royal humour, some of it quite broad. Starting with Elizabeth I's rejoinder to the Earl of Oxford (returning after years of self-imposed exile in shame at having broken wind in the royal presence) 'My Lord, we had forgot the fart', some royal figures – some very unlikely royal figures – have quipped with the best. We must stray for a moment outside the British Royal Family and contemplate the figure of Kaiser Wilhelm II of Germany – the Kaiser Bill of countless cartoons. It is not easy to get laughs if your audience is laughing at you already, so a man in a *Pickelhaube* starts at a disadvantage. However, in 1917, when he heard that the British Royal Family had changed its name to Windsor, his instant reaction was 'I look forward to the next performance of *The Merry Wives of Saxe-Coburg-Gotha*.' Not bad for a chap handicapped by the silliest hat and silliest moustache in history, but full marks to him: it is difficult to think of a category of beings promising less merriment.

'My Lord, we had forgot the fart' rebounded on Elizabeth's successor and namesake, the present Queen Elizabeth. Driving in an open carriage on a state occasion to welcome a foreign potentate, the rear horse lifted its tail and broke wind, prodigiously. It was difficult to ignore, so Her Majesty tendered her apologies to her guest.

'Oh, please don't apologise,' he said. 'I thought it was the horse.'

It must immediately be admitted that Queen Victoria – in modern parlance – 'didn't do jokes'. Apparently she could laugh very heartily. When she asked Admiral Foley how his sister was, the Admiral took her to be asking about HMS *Eurydice*, a recently salvaged frigate. 'Well, ma'am, I'm going to turn her over, take a good look at her bottom and have it scraped,' bellowed the old sea dog. On this occasion Queen Victoria *was* amused, and had to hide her face. But laughing is not making jokes, and besides this anecdote has the ring of a manufactured story.

('We are not amused' is variously ascribed to reproving her children for making a vulgar joke; and to reproving the Brigade of Guards for playing 'Colonel Bogey' during the trooping of the colour. The second possibility depends on the Queen's knowing that the word 'Bollocks!' is frequently repeated in the sung version – unlikely – and – less unlikely – on her returning from the dead, since the march was not written until 1914. It is also attributed to an occasion when she saw a trooper of the Horse Guards attempting to imitate her.)

Neither was her son, Edward VII, noted for his wit, though he, too, had his moments. He served sixty years as the Prince of Wales, and must sometimes have wondered if his imperishable mother might outlive him. In 1897, after the singing of 'Eternal Father strong to save' at the Queen's Diamond Jubilee service, he said to the Archbishop of Canterbury, 'It's all very well about the eternal father, but what about my eternal mother?' And when his mother was, eventually, dying he was asked by a courtier if she would be happy in heaven. 'I don't know,' he replied. 'She will have to walk behind the angels, and she won't like that.' (Similar misgivings were voiced by her favourite prime minister, Benjamin Disraeli, on his own death bed.

Asked if he would appreciate a visit from the Queen he said: 'No it is better not. She would only ask me to take a message to Albert.')

The keynote of Edward VII's life was the pleasures of the flesh, and voluptuaries are not often great wits. His record of self-indulgence, both as the Prince of Wales, and as King is impressive. The huge meals, the cigars, the brandy, but above all the tally of mistresses set him far apart from his mother, Queen Victoria, and his son, George V. He should really be our Merry Monarch Mark II, but he lacked Charles II's easy-going nature, and his style. He early attracted his mother's censure – 'Why, I caught him smoking only a fortnight after his dear father died' – and went on attracting it throughout her reign. He had the good fortune to marry Princess Alexandra of Denmark, a beauty and apparently tolerant of her husband's multiple infidelities, referring to him as 'My naughty little man'. Her tolerance may not have stretched as far as that remark suggests. In 1910, as her husband's body was lying in state, she said to Lord Esher 'Now at least I know where he is.'

And his grandson, Edward VIII, in spite of a similarly naughty reputation, left little behind to trigger a belly laugh, although he was probably the only royal to be caught by the cops in a speakeasy during Prohibition. He escaped by hastily donning the chef's hat and pretending to be one of the kitchen staff. In spite of this

his impressions of America were largely favourable: 'The thing that impresses me most about America is the way the parents obey their children'. (*See* George V immediately below.)

For some of the better royal jokes we must turn to George V. Most modern commentators take his famous last words 'Bugger Bognor' to be apocryphal. I don't like this carping spirit of revisionism. 'Bugger Bognor' is too good to be consigned to myth, and the contending 'How is the Empire?' is too po-faced for words, besides smacking heavily of official propaganda. No. Let the bearded old salt have his Bognor and be famous for it. He is not an easy figure to associate with humour. A severe father – ('My father was frightened of his mother. I was frightened of my father. And I am damned well going to see to it that my children are frightened of me.') – he had a reserved and stuffy exterior. But there are many stories that show him in a more sympathetic light. His stamp collecting has often been cited against him – as if it were an example of a small thing pleasing a small mind. But collecting things is a widespread human foible, and he seemed to take a fairly objective view of it. When one of his aides one remarked to him, 'I see in *The Times* that some damn fool has given fourteen hundred pounds for a single stamp at a private sale', he was met with the reply, 'I am that damn fool.'

Even more likeably, he once asked the American ambassador how long the US President served.

'Four years, sir,' replied the ambassador.

"My God!' the King said. 'If I could get through in four years I'd never run again.'

And can one blame him? In 1935 his Foreign Secretary, Sir Samuel Hoare, signed the Hoare-Laval Pact in Paris, an agreement that virtually handed Abyssinia on a plate to the Italians. Like many others, the King was disgusted. 'No more coals to Newcastle. No more Hoares to Paris,' he commented. And when what you might call the other Hore in his government – Leslie Hore-Belisha – instituted the Belisha beacon at pedestrian crossings, the King told his chauffeur to stop so that he could get out and test one. He returned delighted, and told his chauffeur 'One of my devoted subjects has just called me a doddering old idiot.' (There is a feeling that monarchs enjoy these little outings in the spirit of schoolchildren given a half-holiday. Generally their lives are so hedged in by routine and protocol that their few moments of escape present a spectacle of innocence masquerading as raffishness – like nuns naughtily having a smoke.)

As soon as it became reasonably safe, intellectuals, from Voltaire onwards, have loved to attack and satirise monarchs. George V was no exception, falling foul of H. G. Wells, who accused him of presiding over 'an alien and uninspiring court'. The King was indignant. 'I may be uninspiring, but I'm damned if I'm an alien!'

I would not describe royalty as 'uninspiring'. They often manage to inspire the divine passion in others. While failure to produce issue is the most frequent cause of the extinction of aristocratic dynasties, royalty seems never to suffer from this disability. They appear to be devotedly philoprogenitive people. In 1830, William IV, then the Duke of Clarence, was summoned from his bed to be told that he had inherited the crown. Instead of holding some sort of levee, or making some statement, he returned straight to bed 'to enjoy', he told his wife Adelaide, 'the novelty of sleeping with a Queen.' He had two children by his wife, and ten by his former mistress, the actress Dorothea Jordan. Queen Victoria's enormous tally of offspring speaks for itself, even without her exclamation to the surgeon who informed her that she must have no more children – 'Oh! Sir James! Can I have no more fun in bed?'

Indeed royals tend to attract the opposite sex like jam attracts wasps, and there is something revoltingly goody-goody about Elizabeth Woodville (1437–92) who addressed Edward IV thus: 'My liege, I know I am not good enough to be your queen, but I am far too good to become your mistress.'

Scheming little puss. And – surprise, surprise – she became Queen anyway. The present Prince of Wales has had more than his fair share of trouble with the Female of the Species, starting with the comparatively mild affliction of scantily clad tribal dancers.

'It's become an occupational hazard. You take a deep breath and do it for England.'

And where the fair sex is concerned he is one of those who has been more womanised against than womanising. His great-great-grandfather, Edward VII, set an altogether brisker pace. He had so many mistresses that at his coronation a whole pew in Westminster Abbey had to be set aside for them. Inevitably it became known as 'the loose box'. It all began in 1860 with the famous incident at the Curragh, in Ireland, when an actress was smuggled into the nineteen-year-old Prince's quarters. (The shock of this event, Queen Victoria believed, hastened the death of Prince Albert a few weeks later. At least, that is what she said, but she said other things too. In the wake of Prince Albert's death, after months of thunderous silence, one of her ladies in waiting ventured to say how dreadful it was that His Royal Highness should have died of typhoid fever. The Queen snapped back: 'He did not die of typhoid. He died for lack of what is commonly called pluck' – a remark almost as revealing of the real Victoria as 'Can I have no more fun in bed?')

Edward VII had a particular fondness for actresses, like Lillie Langtry, but eked out the necessarily limited supply of these with more or less anybody who came to hand – the Princesse de Sagan, the Duchesse de Mouchy, sundry commoners in the shape of the demimondaines he encountered on his trips to Paris, and Lady Brooke – Lady 'Babbling' Brooke to her friends. It has been alleged that when Sir William Gordon-Cumming suborned Lady Brooke's affections, the Prince arranged for him to be 'framed' on a charge of cheating at cards (the Tranby Croft scandal) in revenge. There is no evidence for this, and besides, as all followers of the reminiscences of Major-General Sir Harry Flashman know, the real culprit was Elspeth, Lady Flashman, who framed Gordon-Cumming in revenge for . . .

But I digress. Perhaps the Prince's favourite among his mistresses was Alice Keppel, thirty-one years his junior. She had a daughter who, as Violet Trefusis, became the lover of the poet Vita Sackville-West, and said so, loudly. All survivors (if any) of the Anglo-Florentine community will remember that she occasionally stood on her dignity as a daughter of Edward VII, presumably without justification since she was born in 1894, four years before her mother met the King. I've digressed again, so I shall go on. Mrs Keppel's great-granddaughter is now Camilla, Duchess of Cornwall, and married to the present Prince of Wales.

Kinda neat, huh?

I must devote some space to Prince Philip, Duke

of Edinburgh, and the present monarch's consort. In reported volume, his utterances outweigh those of all the other extant royals, and they are frequently controversial. Journalists love him. But very few of them are made in a spirit of blithe innocence. The Duke of Edinburgh has edge. He has attitude. And a sort of unwelcome earthy sanity which is perhaps the obverse of his family background. His mother, Princess Andrew, more widely known as Alice, of Greece, *née* Battenberg, was potty in a way that even the British aristocracy might envy. She consulted the Ouija board, received messages from packs of cards, and once announced that she had a dinner date with Jesus, a date that was obviously successful since she subsequently believed she was enjoying a physical relationship with him. She also believed herself to be magnetic, and claimed to have a group of followers in Bedfordshire. Bedfordshire? So they locked her up in various clinics where she opted to dress as a nun and make faces at the attendants. She spent her last few years in Buckingham Palace, where the staff became rather fond of her.

I mention her to demonstrate that this is just the sort of background that might inoculate a chap against the follies of fashionable thought. And that is exactly what Prince Philip is inoculated against. He is not politically correct.

Speaking to the American ambassador in 2000:

'People think there's a rigid class system here, but dukes have even been known to marry chorus girls. Some have even married Americans.'

Yes! And an incontestable truth from 2002, addressed to the award-winning French chef, Régis Crépy: 'The French don't know how to cook breakfast.'

Better and better. And addressing the Paraguayan dictator, General Stroessner, in 1962: 'It's a pleasure to be in a country that isn't ruled by its people.'

We have lift-off.

You don't have to agree with the Prince to enjoy the blast of fresh air generated by his absolute disregard for the conventional pieties. And there remains the question – are these utterances straightforward gaffes, or are they something more pointed? Surely he was aware that the American ambassador could scarcely relish American womanhood being classed below chorus girls? And that the French are exquisitely sensitive on the subject of their cuisine? And that General Stroessner, like all dictators, revelled in the falsehood that he embodied the people's aspirations (hence his care to secure 98 per cent of the registered vote)?

I think it overwhelmingly likely that the Prince knew all these things, and the clincher is this. In 1997 he was introduced to the German Chancellor, Helmut Kohl, and addressed him as *Reichskanzler*. The last person to bear that title was Adolf Hitler, and it has not been used since 1945. Surely the Prince simply succumbed to temptation? I mean, life is sparing of such opportunities. You have to seize them as they arise. (The only German to whom I have told this story, fell into unseemly mirth and her only coherent utterance was '*Ja*. That Kohl. He thought he was king.')

His wife, the present Queen, Elizabeth II, has played her cards very close to her chest throughout her reign. Her public face is serious, sometimes solemn. It has pleased satirists to present her as domestic and ordinary – 'Brenda' – but she has formidable knowledge and experience and does not scruple to speak her mind. Prime ministers are reported to have left her presence trembling. In the case of several of them, I certainly hope so. She is the reverse of the Higher Lunacy celebrated in this book, but I cannot resist the following.

More or less the worst thing you can do as a naval officer, other than lose your ship to enemy action, is to bend it against something hard and solid – like the mole at the harbour mouth. A senior admiral had committed just such an offence in his early career, and when he was presented at Buckingham Palace to receive his knighthood he felt impelled to own up.

'I'm afraid, Your Majesty, that I was the officer who pranged his ship in Gibraltar harbour.'

'*Whose* ship?' was the cold reply.

I say 'cold', but of course she may have spoken with

twinkling merriment. History does not record. Either way it was an apt put-down.

In the last thirty years the royal family has undergone a process wittily described by the writer Rachel Johnson as 'downward nobility'. They have married commoners. Of course, upon marriage, these people become 'royal', so I think it fair to include them in this chapter. One in particular attracts our attention – Sarah, Duchess of York, *née* Sarah Ferguson. Long before she became royal, or even thought of it, she had to sit a Scripture exam at school, probably nowadays called Religious Education. 'Who was born in a stable and attracted a following of millions?' she was asked.

'Red Rum,' she promptly replied.

If this answer was given honestly, in open-eyed innocence, it is nothing short of magnificent. If knowingly, as a tease, it shows a very pleasing wit. Take your pick. I go for the first option. She has also shown a refreshing candour about the debacle of her marriage.

'I'm doing pretty well considering. In the past, when anyone left the royal family they had you beheaded.'

At the risk of seeming to agree with Mohammed Fayed, I wouldn't entirely put it past Prince Philip.

Perhaps only two recent royals attain the heights of blithe unselfconsciousness that we seek. Here is Queen Geraldine bewailing her exile from the throne of Albania:

'Of course we'll go back there one day. Meanwhile we have to make a new life for ourselves at the Ritz.'

There is also the story, told by Peter Ustinov, of an unnamed relict of some Central European monarchy. She was tacked on to the end of a procession of dignitaries 'meeting the cast' after a royal command performance. As she trailed along at the back she peered earnestly into each actor's face and said, in thick Germanic tones: 'Such a pity about ze Rrrevolution.'

And the last word goes to Queen Mary, when evacuated to Badminton House during the war: 'So *that's* what hay looks like!'

'The noise of one of these little
string and paper machines so
disturbed his peace that he
seized his shotgun, stepped
out onto his lawn, drew a bead
on the offender, and fired. The
machine had to make a crash
landing in the next field.'

AFTERWORD

In the foreword I said that I had not actually invented anything, but I admitted that I had 'depended on my memory', which is often one and the same thing – as my mistaken attribution of the third Lord Tweedsmuir's story (page 144) suggests. And it is not just *my* memory/ imagination. In a genre (anecdote) that depends so heavily on hearsay, other peoples' memories/imaginations also play a part. For example, to my great grief, I can find no other source for Lord Dunsany's shooting two zebras in Piccadilly (page 52) than William Donaldson's *Brewer's Rogues, Villains and Eccentrics*. (A mention on the Web is also clearly derived from Donaldson.) I cannot possibly ignore Lord Dunsany and his two zebras simply because Donaldson's 'memory' might be as unreliable as mine.

I went so far as to write to John Lobb Ltd to ask if the company held any record of the zebra cart, and received this courteous reply from the reigning John Lobb: 'I somehow do not think that my grandmother, who owned the business during the 30s would have advertised in that way. Indeed it has long been our policy never to advertise!' (Lord Rothschild at Tring was among the few to break zebras successfully to harness, and drove them four-in-hand in London. It may be that some rumour about the Tring zebras gave rise to this story.)

If there are no reliable sources for such an indispensable story, what is the conscientious chronicler to do? My duty is clear.

Make that three zebras.

There follow all the anecdotes in this book that depend primarily on my memory, unless already disclosed in the text, with some attempt to explain how they might have got there.

Lord Lonsdale's peregrinations by special trains (page 3) are a memory of a book I once read, title and author now forgotten. I hope I have not confused him with the Marquess of Anglesey. The Duke of Northumberland's disappointment about toast (page 16) I have only by hearsay, and from different sources – strangely enough, always about the same Duke. Anecdotes often get transferred to other likely sources, but not in this case. The rude limerick about The Souls (page 25) has stuck in my mind without any memory of where I heard it. I would like to claim authorship, but someone else will almost certainly recognise and identify it. I would also like to claim authorship of the definition of 'sport', and its distinction from 'games', on page 35, but again I cannot. I pinched it from the writer John Buchan, the first Lord Tweedsmuir. The Master of Foxhounds upbraiding the footballers (pages 36–7) is a memory of something once read. I was told about the Duke of Edinburgh and Lord Mountbatten fishing (page 40) by a ghillie on the neighbouring estate – Ballater – in 1959. I know of no hard evidence that Betty McKeever (pages 41–2) left her body to be fed to her hounds, but two people who knew her as well as I did have told me it was so. She would have loved the idea, anyway, even if she didn't actually do it. General Pitt-Rivers shooting down an aeroplane with a twelve-bore shotgun (page 47) was told me by my uncle, the Rev. Peter Murray, and my authority that John Betjeman spent his wedding celebrations snapping his made-up bow tie at his mother-in-law is the late Bertie Lomas, also a poet. Lord Curzon and 'the lower orders' was told to me by the late Brigadier Peter Young, but the circumstances of our get-togethers were not conducive to serious scholarship, and the details of its provenance – if any – are lost somewhere between the bar of the Savage Club and the bar of the East India and Sports Club. The career of the beautiful Jane Digby is well-documented, but her diary entry for her seventieth birthday was told to me by her descendant, Professor Adrian Digby. Again it was verbal testimony, but I think I have the wording right. The hapless Rector of Stiffkey is also well-covered territory, and if my account seems to lean too heavily on Ronald Blythe's, in his book *The Age of Illusion*, it is because his is by far the best treatment of the subject. The story about Queen Mary and Lord Kitchener cheating each other I heard from my late aunt, Mrs Phoebe Dawes, who claimed to know the lady-in-waiting who conducted the negotiations.

Anecdotes are no more than stories told for amusement – sometimes close to the truth, sometimes far from it; sometimes malicious, sometimes harmless. No one but a blockhead would take them seriously.

BIBLIOGRAPHY

Beaumont, Tim (ed.), *The Selective Ego: The Diaries of James Agate* (London, 1976)

Blackett-Ord, Mark, *Hell-fire Duke: Life of the Duke of Wharton* (Windsor, 1982)

Blythe, Ronald, *The Age of Illusion: England in the Twenties and Thirties, 1919–1940* (London, 1964)

Bolt, Rodney, *As Good as God, as Clever as the Devil: The Impossible Life of Mary Benson* (London, 2011)

Brandreth, Gyles, *Oxford Dictionary of Humorous Quotations* (Oxford, 2013)

Bryson, Bill, *A Short History of Nearly Everything* (London, 2003)

Bryson, Bill, *Notes from a Small Island* (London, 1995)

Byrne, Paula, *Mad World: Evelyn Waugh and the*

Secrets of Brideshead (London, 2009)

Campbell, John, *F. E. Smith: First Earl of Birkenhead* (London, 1983)

Cannadine, David, *Aspects of Aristocracy: Grandeur and Decline in Modern Britain* (New Haven, Conn., 1994)

Concise Dictionary of National Biography (Oxford, 1992)

Cooper, Lady Diana, *The Light of Common Day* (London, 1959)

Cullen, Tom, *The Prostitutes' Padre: The Story of the Notorious Rector of Stiffkey* (London, 1975)

Dampier, Phil, and Walton, Ashley, *Duke of Hazard: The Wit and Wisdom of Prince Philip* (Leicester 2006)

Donaldson, William, *Brewer's Rogues, Villains and Eccentrics: An A–Z of Roguish Britons Through the Ages* (London, 2002)

Douglas-Home, Jamie, *Stately Passions: The Scandals of Britain's Great Houses* (London, 2006)

Edgar, Anne, *Her Master's Voice: The Life of Betty McKeever* (UK, 2000)

Fadiman, Clifton, *The Faber Book of Anecdotes* (London, 1985)

Gilmour, David, *Curzon: Imperial Statesman* (New York, 2003)

Gottlieb, Robert, 'Dah-Ling: The Strange Case of

BIBLIOGRAPHY

Tallulah Bankhead', *The New Yorker* (New York, 2005)

Harris, Captain William Cornwallis, *The Wild Sports of Southern Africa* (1839)

King-Clark, Rex, *Jack Churchill: 'Unlimited Boldness'* (Knutsford, 1997)

Leacock, Stephen, *Moonbeams from the Larger Lunacy* (Montreal, 1915)

Leslie, Anita, *The Marlborough House Set* (London, 1973)

Lovell, Mary S., *A Scandalous Life: The Biography of Jane Digby* (London, 1998)

Martin, Brian P., *The Great Shoots: Britain's Best – Past and Present* (London, 1987)

Michell, John, *Eccentric Lives and Peculiar Notions* (Kempton, Ill., 1999)

Parris, Matthew, *The Great Unfrocked: Two Thousand Years of Church Scandal* (London, 1998)

Portland, William John Arthur Charles James Cavendish-Bentinck, sixth Duke of, *Men, Women and Things: Memories of the Duke of Portland* (London, 1937)

Ransom, Teresa, *The Mysterious Miss Marie Corelli: Queen of Victorian Bestsellers* (Stroud, 1999)

Roberts, Stephen, and Acton, Mark, *The Parliamentary Career of Charles De Laet Waldo Sibthorp 1826–55: Ultra Tory Opposition to Reform in Nineteenth*

Century Britain (New York, 2010)

Rose, Kenneth, *The Later Cecils* (London, 1975)

Ruffer, Jonathan G., *The Big Shots: Edwardian Shooting Parties* (London, 2002)

Sutherland, Douglas, *The English Gentleman* (London, 1978)

Wardrop, Major A. E., *Modern Pig-Sticking* (London, 1914)

Westminster, Loelia Grosvenor, Duchess of, *Grace and Favour: The Memoirs of Loelia, Duchess of Westminster* (London, 1961)

Wilson, Nancy R., *Queen of Speed: The Racy Life of Mary Petre Bruce* (Bradford-on-Avon, 2012)

Wintle, Alfred D., *The Last Englishman: An Autobiography of Lieut.-Col. Alfred Daniel Wintle, M.C. (1st The Royal Dragoons)* (London, 1968)

Wintle, Justin, and Kenin, Richard (eds), *Dictionary of Biographical Quotation* (London, 1978)

Ziegler, Philip, *Diana Cooper: The Biography of Lady Diana Cooper* (London, 1981)

Wikipedia, the free encyclopedia:
https://www.wikipedia.org

INDEX

INDEX

MAD TOFFS